MEDICAL
TECHNICIANS

FOURTH EDITION

Ferguson

An imprint of ✓®Facts On File

Careers in Focus: Medical Technicians, Fourth Edition

Copyright © 2004 by Facts On File, Inc.

Ferguson
An imprint of Facts On File, Inc.
132 West 31st Street
New York NY 10001

Careers in focus. Medical Technicians. — 4th ed.
   p. cm.
Includes bibliographical references and index.
   ISBN 0-8160-5554-8 (alk. paper)
   1. Medical technology—Vocational guidance. 2. Vocational guidance. I. Title:
Medical technicians. II. J.G. Ferguson Publishing Company.
R855.3.C36 2004
610'.28—dc22   2003026177

Ferguson books are available at special discounts when purchased in bulk quantities for businesses, associations, institutions, or sales promotions. Please call our Special Sales Department in New York at (212) 967-8800 or (800) 322-8755.

You can find Ferguson on the World Wide Web at http://www.fergpubco.com

Text design by David Strelecky

Printed in the United States of America

MP FOF 10 9 8 7 6 5 4 3 2 1

This book is printed on acid-free paper.

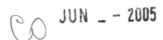

Table of Contents

Introduction

Technicians are highly specialized workers who work with scientists, physicians, engineers, and other professionals, as well as with clients and customers. They assist professionals in many activities, and they frequently direct skilled workers. They work in factories, businesses, science labs, hospitals, law offices, clinics, shops, and private homes. Some work for themselves as consultants. They are found in all facets of the work world and make up one of the fastest growing career sectors.

The health care industry employs many technicians. Modern medicine is increasingly dependent on sophisticated machinery to help make diagnoses, provide effective treatments, and keep the body functioning while patients are undergoing surgery. Many of these machines require the special skills of medical technicians to operate properly. The careers in this book represent a wide range of job opportunities found in the technical side of the health care field. Because of this variety, you will find that there are varying educational requirements, salaries, and advancement opportunities associated with these careers.

An example of the evolving role of medical technology is in the area of heart disease. Physicians can now order a number of tests to detect heart disease more definitively and at a much earlier stage. These include tests that pick up heart sounds and murmurs (phonocardiology), tests that record the heart's electrical activity (vector cardiography), stress tests, ultrasound tests (echocardiography), and procedures such as cardiac catheterization, in which a tube is inserted into a patient's heart to detect blockages.

Medical technicians assist physicians in some tests, such as the cardiac catheterization procedure, but most technicians conduct tests themselves and pass the results on to physicians for interpretation. Some technicians, such as dialysis technicians and respiratory therapy technicians, see patients all day every day, while others, such as medical and dental laboratory technicians, spend all their time in laboratories and rarely see patients at all.

Technician careers are appealing for a very practical reason: They are a fast track to a good job. For someone who is interested in medicine but who wants neither the educational commitment nor full responsibilities of being a doctor, a career as a medical technician may be a good option. Most technician positions require at least one year of postsecondary training, although a few demand even less. Dialysis technicians, for example, are usually trained on the job, and emergency medical technicians must complete a 110-hour course. At the other end of the spectrum is the job of medical technologist, which requires a minimum of a bachelor's degree. The minimum education requirement for the vast majority of technician positions is a one- to two-year certificate program or associate's degree, but a bachelor's degree generally gives job candidates an edge on the competition and guarantees a better salary and increased opportunity for advancement.

According to U.S. government projections, the health care industry will create approximately 2.8 million new jobs by 2010. Employment in health care is projected to increase 25 percent during this period. Medical technicians will continue to be in high demand, especially since the emphasis on preventive care requires more physicals and more tests.

Each article in *Careers in Focus: Medical Technicians* discusses a particular medical technician occupation in detail. The articles appear in Ferguson's *Encyclopedia of Careers and Vocational Guidance.* All articles have been updated and revised since the last edition of this book with the latest information from the U.S. Department of Labor and other sources. Throughout the book you will also find informative sidebars, interviews with people working in the medical field, and illustrative photos of some of the careers.

The **Quick Facts** section provides a brief summary of the career including recommended school subjects, personal skills, work environment, minimum educational requirements, salary ranges, certification or licensing requirements, and employment outlook. This section also provides acronyms and identification numbers for the following government classification indexes: the *Dictionary of Occupational Titles* (DOT), the *Guide for Occupational Exploration* (GOE), the National Occupational Classification (NOC) Index, and the Occupational Information Network (O*NET)-Standard Occupational Classification System (SOC) index. The DOT, GOE, and O*NET-SOC indexes have been created by the U.S. government; the NOC index is Canada's career classification system. Readers can use the identification numbers listed in the Quick Facts section to access further information on a career. Print editions of the DOT (*Dictionary of Occupational Titles.* Indianapolis, Ind.: JIST Works, 1991) and GOE (*The Complete Guide for Occupational Exploration.* Indianapolis, Ind.: JIST Works, 1993) are available at libraries, and electronic versions of the NOC (http://www23.hrdc-drhc.gc.ca/2001/e/generic/welcome.shtml) and O*NET-SOC (http://online.onetcenter.org) are available on the World Wide Web. When no DOT, GOE, NOC, or O*NET-SOC numbers are present, this means that the U.S. Department of Labor or the Human Resources Development Canada have not created a numerical designation for this career. In this instance, you will see the acronym "N/A," or not available.

The **Overview** section is a brief introductory description of the duties and responsibilities of someone in the career. Oftentimes, a career may have a variety of job titles. When this is the case, alternative career titles are presented in this section.

The **History** section describes the history of the particular career as it relates to the overall development of its industry or field.

The Job describes the primary and secondary duties of the career.

Requirements discusses high school and postsecondary education and training requirements, any certification or licensing necessary, and any other personal requirements for success in the career.

Exploring offers suggestions on how to gain some experience in or knowledge of the particular job before making a firm educational and financial commitment. The focus is on what can be done while still in high school (or in the early years of college) to gain a better understanding of the career.

The **Employers** section gives an overview of typical places of employment for the job.

Starting Out discusses the best ways to land that first job, be it through the college placement office, newspaper ads, or personal contact.

The **Advancement** section describes what kind of career path to expect from the career and how to get on it.

Earnings lists salary ranges and describes the typical fringe benefits.

The **Work Environment** section describes the typical surroundings and conditions of employment—whether indoors or outdoors, noisy or quiet, social or independent, and so on. Also discussed are typical hours worked, any seasonal fluctuations, and the stresses and strains of the job.

The **Outlook** section summarizes the career in terms of the general economy and industry projections. For the most part, Outlook information is obtained from the Bureau of Labor Statistics and is supplemented by information taken from professional associations. Job growth terms follow those used in the *Occupational Outlook Handbook*. Growth described as "much faster than the average" means an increase of 36 percent or more. Growth described as "faster than the average" means an increase of 21–35 percent. Growth described as "about as fast as the average" means an increase of 10–20 percent. Growth described as "little change or more slowly than the average" means an increase of 0–9 percent. "Decline" means a decrease of 1 percent or more.

Each article ends with **For More Information**, which lists organizations that can provide career information on training, education, internships, scholarships, and job placement.

If you have a keen interest in health, science, and technology and a genuine desire to be of service to other people, then a career as a medical technician might be right for you. Take the time to read about all of the careers in this diverse and changing field, and be sure to contact the various organizations for more information.

Biomedical Equipment Technicians

QUICK FACTS

School Subjects
Biology
Technical/shop

Personal Skills
Mechanical/manipulative
Technical/scientific

Work Environment
Primarily indoors
Primarily one location

Minimum Education Level
Associate's degree

Salary Range
$20,000 to $35,340 to
$44,000

Certification or Licensing
Recommended

Outlook
About as fast as the average

DOT
639

GOE
02.04.02

NOC
N/A

O*NET-SOC
49-9062.00, 51-9082.00

OVERVIEW

Biomedical equipment technicians handle the complex medical equipment and instruments found in hospitals, clinics, and research facilities. This equipment is used for medical therapy and diagnosis and includes heart-lung machines, artificial kidney machines, patient monitors, chemical analyzers, and other electrical, electronic, mechanical, or pneumatic devices.

Technicians' main duties are to inspect, maintain, repair, and install this equipment. They disassemble equipment to locate malfunctioning components, repair or replace defective parts, and reassemble the equipment, adjusting and calibrating it to ensure that it operates according to manufacturers' specifications. Other duties of biomedical equipment technicians include modifying equipment according to the directions of medical or supervisory personnel, arranging with equipment manufacturers for necessary equipment repair, and safety-testing equipment to ensure that patients, equipment operators, and other staff members are safe from electrical or mechanical hazards. Biomedical equipment technicians work with hand tools, power tools, measuring devices, and manufacturers' manuals.

Technicians may work for equipment manufacturers as salespeople or as service technicians, or for a health care facility specializing in the repair or maintenance of specific equipment, such as that used in radiology, nuclear medicine, or patient monitoring. In the United States, approximately 28,000 people work as biomedical equipment technicians.

HISTORY

Today's complex biomedical equipment is the result of advances in three different areas of engineering and scientific research. The first is medicine's ever-increasing knowledge of the human body and of the disease processes that afflict it. Although the accumulation of medical knowledge has been going on for thousands of years, most of the discoveries leading to the development of medical technology have occurred during the last 300 years. During the past 100 years especially, we have learned a great deal about the chemical and electrical nature of the human body.

The second contribution to biomedical technology's development is the field of instrumentation—the design and building of precision measuring devices. Throughout the history of medicine, physicians and medical researchers have tried to learn about and to monitor the workings of the human body with whatever instruments were available to them. However, instruments that could detect the human body's many subtle and rapid processes were not developed until the industrial revolution of the 18th and 19th.

The third area is mechanization and automation. Biomedical equipment often relies on mechanisms, such as pumps, motors, bellows, control arms, and so forth. These kinds of equipment were initially developed and improved during the industrial revolution, but it was not until the 1950s that the field of medical technology began incorporating the use of automation. During the 1950s, researchers developed machines for analyzing the various components of blood and for preparing tissue specimens for microscopic examination. Probably the most dramatic development of this period was the introduction of the heart-lung machine by John Haysham Gibbon of Philadelphia in 1953, a project he had been working on since 1937.

Since the 1950s, the growth of biomedical technology has been especially dramatic. Thirty years ago, even the most advanced hospitals had only a few pieces of electronic medical equipment; today such hospitals have thousands. The biomedical equipment technician, who services this equipment, has become an important member of the health care delivery team.

In a sense, biomedical equipment technicians represent the newest stage in the history of technicians. The first technicians were skilled assistants who had learned a trade and gone to work for an engineer or scientist. The second generation learned a technology, such as electronics. The most recent generation of technicians needs integrated instruction and competence in at least two fields of science and technology. For the biomedical equipment technician, the fields may vary, but they will most often be electronics and human physiology.

THE JOB

Biomedical equipment technicians are an important link between technology and medicine. They repair, calibrate, maintain, and operate biomedical equipment and work under the supervision of researchers, biomedical engineers, physicians, surgeons, and other professional health care providers.

Repairing faulty instruments is one of the chief functions of biomedical equipment technicians. They investigate equipment problems, determine the extent of malfunctions, make repairs on instruments that have had minor breakdowns, and expedite the repair of instruments with major breakdowns, for instance, by writing an analysis of the problem for the factory. In doing this work, technicians rely on manufacturers' diagrams, maintenance manuals, and standard and specialized test instruments, such as oscilloscopes and pressure gauges.

Installing equipment is another important function of biomedical equipment technicians. They inspect and test new equipment to make sure it complies with performance and safety standards as described in the manufacturer's manuals and diagrams, and as noted on the purchase order. Technicians may also check on proper installation of the equipment, or, in some cases, install it themselves. To ensure safe

Did You Know?

The following are just some of the machines and equipment with which biomedical equipment technicians work:

- patient monitors
- heart-lung machines
- kidney machines
- blood-gas analyzers
- spectrophotometers
- X-ray units
- radiation monitors
- defibrillators
- anesthesia apparatus
- pacemakers
- blood pressure transducers

- spirometers
- sterilizers
- diathermy equipment
- patient-care computers
- ultrasound machines
- CT (computed tomography) scan machines
- PETT (positive emission transaxial tomography) scanners
- MRI (magnetic resonance imaging) machines

operations, technicians need a thorough knowledge of the regulations related to the proper grounding of equipment, and they need to actively carry out all steps and procedures to ensure safety.

Maintenance is the third major area of responsibility for biomedical equipment technicians. In doing this work, technicians try to catch problems before they become more serious. To this end, they take apart and reassemble devices, test circuits, clean and oil moving parts, and replace worn parts. They also keep complete records of all machine repairs, maintenance checks, and expenses.

In all three of these areas, a large part of technicians' work consists of consulting with physicians, administrators, engineers, and other professionals. For example, they may be called upon to assist hospital administrators who are making decisions about the repair, replacement, or purchase of new equipment. They consult with medical and research staffs to determine that equipment is functioning safely and properly. They also consult with medical and engineering staffs when called upon to modify or develop equipment. In all of these activities, they use their knowledge of electronics, medical terminology, human anatomy and physiology, chemistry, and physics.

In addition, biomedical equipment technicians are involved in a range of other related duties. Some biomedical equipment technicians maintain inventories of all instruments in the hospital, their condition, location, and operators. They reorder parts and components, assist in providing people with emergency instruments, restore unsafe or defective instruments to working order, and check for safety regulation compliance.

Other biomedical equipment technicians help physicians, surgeons, nurses, and researchers conduct procedures and experiments. In addition, they must be able to explain to staff members how to operate these machines, the conditions under which certain apparatus may or may not be used, how to solve small operating problems, and how to monitor and maintain equipment.

In many hospitals, technicians are assigned to a particular service, such as pediatrics, surgery, or renal medicine. These technicians become specialists in certain types of equipment. However, unlike electrocardiograph technicians or dialysis technicians, who specialize in one kind of equipment, most biomedical equipment technicians must be thoroughly familiar with a large variety of instruments. They might be called upon to prepare an artificial kidney or to work with a blood-gas analyzer. Biomedical equipment technicians also maintain pulmonary function machines. These machines are used in clinics for ambulatory patients, hospital laboratories, departments of medicine for diagnosis and treatment, and rehabilitation of cardiopulmonary patients.

While most biomedical equipment technicians are trained in electronics technology, there is also a need for technicians trained in plastics to work on the development of artificial organs and for people trained in glass blowing to help make the precision parts for specialized equipment.

Many biomedical equipment technicians work for medical instrument manufacturers. These technicians consult and assist in the construction of new machinery, helping to make decisions concerning materials and construction methods to be used in the manufacture of the equipment.

REQUIREMENTS

High School

There are a number of classes you can take in high school to help you prepare for this work. Science classes, such as chemistry, biology, and physics, will give you the science background you will need for working in a medical environment. Take shop classes that deal with electronics, drafting, or blueprint reading. These classes will give you experience working with your hands, following printed directions, using electricity, and working with machinery. Mathematics classes will help you become comfortable working with numbers and formulas. English classes will help you develop your communication skills, which will be important to have when you deal with a variety of different people in your professional life.

Postsecondary Training

To become qualified for this work, you will need to complete postsecondary education that leads either to an associate's degree from a two-year institution or a bachelor's degree from a four-year college or university. Most biomedical equipment technicians choose to receive an associate's degree. Biomedical equipment technology is a relatively new program in some schools and may also be referred to as medical electronics technology or biomedical engineering technology. No matter what the name of the program is, however, you should expect to receive instruction in such areas as anatomy, physiology, electrical and electronic fundamentals, chemistry, physics, and biomedical equipment construction and design. In addition, you will study safety methods in health care facilities and medical equipment troubleshooting, as it will be your job to be the problem solver. You should also expect to continue taking communication or English classes since communications skills will be essential to your work. In addition to the classroom work, many programs often provide you with practical experience in repairing and servicing equipment in a clinical or laboratory setting under the supervision of an experienced equipment technician. In this way, you learn about electrical components and circuits, the design and construction of common pieces of machinery, and computer technology as it applies to biomedical equipment.

By studying various pieces of equipment, you learn a problem-solving technique that applies not only to the equipment studied, but also to equipment you have not yet seen, and even to equipment that has not yet been invented. Part of this problem-solving technique includes learning how and where to locate sources of information.

Some biomedical equipment technicians receive their training in the armed forces. During the course of an enlistment period of four years or less, military personnel can receive training that prepares them for entry-level or sometimes advanced-level positions in the civilian workforce.

Certification or Licensing

The Association for the Advancement of Medical Instrumentation (AAMI), affiliated with the International Certification Commission for Clinical Engineering and Biomedical Technology, issues a certificate for biomedical equipment technicians (called CBET) that is issued based on a written examination, work experience, and educational preparation. In some cases, the educational requirements for certification may be waived for technicians with appropriate employment experience. Although certification is not required for employment, it is highly recommended. Technicians with certification have demonstrated that they have attained an overall knowledge of the field and are dedicated to their profession. Many employers prefer to hire technicians who have this certification.

Other Requirements

Biomedical equipment technicians need mechanical ability and should enjoy working with tools. Because this job demands quick decision making and prompt repair work, technicians should work well under pressure. You should also be extremely precise in your work, have good communications skills, and enjoy helping others—an essential quality for anyone working in the health care industry.

EXPLORING

You will have difficulty gaining any direct experience in biomedical equipment technology until you are in a training program or working professionally. Your first hands-on opportunities generally come in the clinical and laboratory phases of your education. You can, however, visit school and community libraries to seek out books written about careers in medical technology. You can also join a club devoted to chemistry, biology, radio equipment, or electronics.

Perhaps the best way to learn more about this job is to set up, with the help of teachers or guidance counselors, a visit to a local health care facility or to arrange for a biomedical technician to speak to interested students, either on-site or at a career-exploration seminar hosted by the school. You may be able to ask the technician about his or her educational background, what a day on the job is like, and what new technologies are on the horizon. Try to visit a school offering a program in biomedical equipment technology and discuss your career plans with an admissions counselor there. The counselor may also be able to provide you with helpful insights about the career and your preparation for it.

Finally, because this work involves the health care field, consider getting a part-time job or volunteering at a local hospital. Naturally, you won't be asked to work with the biomedical equipment, but you will have the opportunity to see professionals on the job and experience being in the medical environment. Even if your duty is only to escort patients to their tests, you may gain a greater understanding of this work.

EMPLOYERS

Many schools place students in part-time hospital positions to help them gain practical experience. Students are often able to return to these hospitals for full-time employment after graduation. Other places of employment include research institutes and biomedical equipment manufacturers. Government hospitals and the military are also employers of biomedical equipment technicians.

STARTING OUT

Most schools offering programs in biomedical equipment technology work closely with local hospitals and industries, and school placement officers are usually informed about openings when they become available. In some cases, recruiters may visit a school periodically to conduct interviews. Also, many schools place students in part-time hospital jobs to help them gain practical experience. Students are often able to return to these hospitals for full-time employment after graduation.

Another effective method of finding employment is to write directly to hospitals, research institutes, or biomedical equipment manufacturers. Other good sources of leads for job openings include state employment offices and newspaper want ads.

ADVANCEMENT

With experience, biomedical equipment technicians can expect to work with less supervision, and in some cases they may find themselves supervising less-experienced technicians. They may advance to positions in which they serve as instructors, assist in research, or have administrative duties. Although many supervisory positions are open to biomedical equipment technicians, some positions are not available without additional education. In large metropolitan hospitals, for instance, the minimum educational requirement for biomedical engineers, who do much of the supervising of biomedical equipment technicians, is a bachelor's degree; many engineers have a master's degree as well.

EARNINGS

Salaries for biomedical equipment technicians vary in different institutions and localities and according to the experience, training, certification, and type of work done by the technician. According to the U.S. Department of Labor, the median hourly wage for medical equipment repairers was $16.99 in 2000. A technician earning this amount and working full time would have a yearly salary of approximately $35,340. A March 2000 AAMI survey of schools providing biomedical equipment training contained salary figures for their graduates. The average annual salary for graduates of two-year programs listed in the survey was approximately $28,200. At the low end of the salary ranges provided by these schools, graduates had yearly earnings of $20,000; at the high end of the salary ranges, some graduates reported earnings of $44,000. In general, biomedical equipment technicians who work for manufacturers have higher earnings than those who work for hospitals. Naturally, those in supervisory or senior positions also command higher salaries. Benefits, such as health insurance and vacation days, vary with the employer.

WORK ENVIRONMENT

Working conditions for biomedical equipment technicians vary according to employer and type of work done. Hospital employees generally work a 40-hour week; their schedules sometimes include weekends and holidays, and some technicians may be on call for emergencies. Technicians working for equipment manufacturers may have to do extensive traveling to install or service equipment.

The physical surroundings in which biomedical equipment technicians work may vary from day to day. Technicians may work in a lab or treatment room with patients or consult with engineers, administrators, and other staff members. Other days, technicians may spend most of their time at a workbench repairing equipment.

OUTLOOK

Because of the increasing use of electronic medical devices and other sophisticated biomedical equipment, there is a steady demand for skilled and trained biomedical equipment technicians. The U.S. Department of Labor predicts employment for this group to grow about as fast as the average through 2010.

In hospitals the need for more biomedical equipment technicians exists not only because of the increasing use of biomedical equipment but also because hospital administrators realize that these technicians can help hold down costs. Biomedical equipment technicians do this through their preventive maintenance checks and by taking over some routine activities of engineers and administrators, thus releasing those professionals for activities that only they can perform. Through the coming decades, cost containment will remain a high priority for hospital administrators, and as long as biomedical equipment technicians can contribute to that effort, the demand for them should remain strong.

For the many biomedical equipment technicians who work for companies that build, sell, lease, or service biomedical equipment, job opportunities should also continue to grow.

The federal government employs biomedical equipment technicians in its hospitals, research institutes, and the military. Employment in these areas will depend largely on levels of government spending. In the research area, spending levels may vary; however, in health care delivery, spending should remain high for the near future.

FOR MORE INFORMATION

For information on student memberships, biomedical technology programs, and certification, contact
Association for the Advancement of Medical Instrumentation
1110 North Glebe Road, Suite 220
Arlington, VA 22201-4795
Tel: 800-332-2264
http://www.aami.org

Cardiovascular Technologists

OVERVIEW

Cardiovascular technologists assist physicians in diagnosing and treating heart and blood vessel ailments. Depending on their specialties, they operate electrocardiograph machines, perform Holter monitor and stress testing, and assist in cardiac catheterization procedures and ultrasound testing. These tasks help the physicians diagnose heart disease and monitor progress during treatment. Cardiovascular technologists hold approximately 39,000 jobs in the United States.

HISTORY

Electrocardiography can be traced back 300 years to the work of the Dutch anatomist and physiologist Jan Swammerdam, who in 1678 demonstrated that a frog's leg will contract when stimulated with an electrical current. It was not until 1856, however, that two German anatomists, Albert von Kolliker and Heinrich M. Mueller, showed that when a frog's heart contracted, it produced a small electrical current. In succeeding years, the electrical behavior of beating hearts was extensively studied, but always with the chest open and the heart exposed.

In 1887, Augustus Desire Waller discovered that the electrical current of the human heart could be measured with the chest closed. He was able to do this by placing one electrode on a person's chest and another on the person's back and connecting them to a monitoring device. In 1903 Willem Einthoven, a Dutch professor of physiology, perfected the monitoring device so that even the faintest currents from the heart could be detected and recorded graphically.

Throughout the rest of the 20th century, medical researchers made further advancements and refinements on this machine. By the 1940s, for instance, portable electrocardiographs were in use, allowing electrocardiograms to be made in a physician's office or at a patient's bedside. During the 1960s, computerized electrocardiographs were developed to aid physicians in the interpretation of test results. Today, electrocardiographs are widely used in routine physicals, in presurgical physicals, in diagnosing disease, and in monitoring the effects of prescribed therapy. The wide use of these devices ensures a continuing need for trained personnel to operate them.

THE JOB

Technologists who assist physicians in the diagnosis and treatment of heart disease are known as cardiovascular technologists. (*Cardio* means heart; *vascular* refers to the blood vessel/circulatory system.) Increasingly, hospitals are centralizing cardiovascular services under one full cardiovascular "service line" overseen by the same administrator. In addition to cardiovascular technologists, the cardiovascular team at a hospital may include radiology (X-ray) technologists, nuclear medicine technologists, nurses, physician assistants, respiratory technicians, and respiratory therapists. For their part, the cardiovascular technologists contribute by performing one or more of a wide range of procedures in cardiovascular medicine, including invasive (enters a body cavity or interrupts normal body functions), noninvasive, peripheral vascular, or echocardiography (ultrasound) procedures. In most facilities, technologists use equipment that is among the most advanced in the medical field; drug therapies also may be used as part of the diagnostic imaging procedures or in addition to them. Technologists' services may be required when the patient's condition is first being explored, before surgery, during surgery (cardiology technologists primarily), or during rehabilitation of the patient. Some of the work is performed on an outpatient basis.

Depending on their specific areas of skill, some cardiovascular technologists are employed in nonhospital health care facilities. For example, they may work for clinics, mobile medical services, or private doctors' offices. Much of their equipment can go just about anywhere.

Some of the specific duties of cardiovascular technologists are described in the following paragraphs. Exact titles of these technologists often vary from medical facility to medical facility because there is no standardized naming system. *Electrocardiograph technologists,* or *EKG technologists,* use an electrocardiograph machine to detect the electronic impulses that come from a patient's heart. The EKG machine records these signals on a paper graph called an *electrocardiogram.* The electronic impulses recorded by the EKG machine can tell the physician about the action of the heart during and between the individual heartbeats. This in turn reveals important information about the condition of the heart, including irregular heartbeats or the presence of blocked arteries, which the physician can use to diagnose heart disease, monitor progress during treatment, or check the patient's condition after recovery.

To use an EKG machine, the technologist attaches electrodes (small, disklike devices about the size of a silver dollar) to the patient's chest. Wires attached to the electrodes lead to the EKG machine. Twelve or more leads may be attached. To get a better reading from the electrodes, the technologist may first apply an adhesive gel to the patient's skin that helps to conduct the electrical impulses. The technologist then operates controls on the EKG machine or (more commonly) enters commands for the machine into a computer. The electrodes pick up the electronic signals from the heart and transmit them to the EKG machine. The machine registers and makes a printout of the signals, with a stylus (pen) recording their pattern on a long roll of graph paper.

During the test, the technologist may move the electrodes in order to get readings of electrical activity in different parts of the heart muscle. Since EKG equipment can be sensitive to electrical impulses from other sources, such as other parts of the patient's body or equipment in the room where the EKG test is being done, the technologist must watch for false readings.

After the test, the EKG technologist takes the electrocardiogram off the machine, edits it or makes notes on it, and sends it to the physician (usually a cardiologist, or heart specialist). Physicians may have computer assistance to help them use and interpret the electrocardiogram; special software is available to assist them with their diagnoses.

EKG technologists do not have to repair EKG machines, but they do have to keep an eye on them and know when they are malfunctioning so they can call someone for repairs. They also may keep the machines stocked with paper. Of all the cardiovascular technical positions, EKG technologist positions are the most numerous.

Holter monitoring and stress testing may be performed by *Holter monitor technologists* or *stress test technologists,* respectively, or they may be additional duties of some EKG technologists. In *Holter monitoring,* electrodes are fastened to the patient's chest, and a small, portable monitor is strapped to the patient's body, often at the waist. The small monitor contains a magnetic tape or cassette that records the action of the heart during activity—as the patient moves, sits, stands, sleeps, etc. The patient is required to wear the Holter monitor for 24–48 hours while he or she goes about normal daily activities. When the patient returns to the hospital, the technologist removes the magnetic tape or cassette from the monitor and puts it in a scanner to produce audio and visual representations of heart activity. (Hearing how the heart sounds during activity helps physicians diagnose a possible heart condition.) The technologist reviews and analyzes the information revealed in the tape. Finally, the technologist may print out the parts of the tape that show abnormal heart patterns or make a full tape for the physician.

Stress tests record the heart's performance during physical activity. In one type of stress test, the technologist connects the patient to the EKG machine, attaching electrodes to the patient's arms, legs, and chest, and obtains a reading of the patient's resting heart activity and blood pressure. Then, the patient is asked to walk on a treadmill for a designated period of time while the technologist and the physician monitor the heart. The treadmill speed is increased so that the technologist and physician can see what happens when the heart is put under higher levels of exertion.

Cardiology technologists specialize in providing support for *cardiac catheterization* (tubing) procedures. These procedures are classified as invasive because they require the physician and attending technologists to enter a body cavity or interrupt normal body functions. In one cardiac catheterization procedure—an *angiogram*—a catheter (tube) is inserted into the heart (usually by way of a blood vessel in the leg) in order to see the condition of the heart blood vessels, whether there is a blockage. In another procedure, known as *angioplasty,* a catheter with a balloon at the end is inserted into an artery to widen it. According to the American Heart Association's 2001 Heart and Stroke Statistical Update, 1,069,000 angioplasties were done in the United States in 1999. Of these, 601,000 were percutaneous transluminal coronary angioplasties. Cardiology technologists also perform a variety of other procedures.

Unlike some of the other cardiovascular technologists, cardiology technologists actually assist in surgical procedures. They may help secure the patient to the table, set up a 35mm video camera or other imaging device under the instructions of the physician (to produce images that assist the physician in guiding the catheter through the cardiovascular system), enter into a computer information about the surgical procedure (as it is taking place), and provide other support.

After the procedure, the technologist may process the angiographic film for use by the physician. Cardiology technologists may also assist during open-heart surgery by preparing and monitoring the patient and placing or monitoring pacemakers.

Vascular technologists and *echocardiographers* are specialists in noninvasive cardiovascular procedures and use ultrasound equipment to obtain and record information about the condition of the heart. Ultrasound equipment is used to send out sound waves to the area of the body being studied; when the sound waves hit the part being studied, they send echoes to the ultrasound machine. The echoes are "read" by the machine, which creates an image on a monitor, permitting the technologist to get an instant "image" of the part of the body and its condition. Vascular technologists are specialists in the use of ultrasound equipment to study blood flow and circulation problems. Echocardiographers are specialists in the use of ultrasound equipment to evaluate the heart and its structures, such as the valves.

The Facts on Blood Pressure

A blood-pressure reading consists of two numbers: one that measures the force in the arteries when the heart beats (systolic pressure) and one that measures the force in the arteries when the heart is at rest (diastolic pressure). When a person has high blood pressure (also called hypertension) they are at higher risk for different kinds of heart disease. Thus, it is important for all people to have their blood pressure checked regularly, especially if they are over 35 years of age. Fortunately, high blood pressure can be controlled through healthy diet, exercise, and prescription medications. Check with your family doctor or school nurse for more information on blood pressure.

The following are the American Medical Association's recommended blood pressure levels.

Blood Pressure Category	Systolic		Diastolic
Normal	less than 120	AND	less than 80
Prehypertension	120–139	OR	80–89
High, Stage 1	140–159	OR	90–99
High, Stage 2	160 or higher	OR	100 or higher

Cardiac monitor technicians are similar to and sometimes perform some of the same duties as EKG technologists. Usually working in the intensive care unit or cardio-care unit of the hospital, cardiac monitor technicians keep watch over the patient, monitoring screens to detect any sign that a patient's heart is not beating as it should. Cardiac monitor technicians begin their shift by reviewing the patient's records to familiarize themselves with what the patient's normal heart rhythms should be, what the current pattern is, and what types of problems have been observed. Throughout the shift, cardiac monitor technicians watch for heart rhythm irregularities that need prompt medical attention. Should there be any, they notify a nurse or doctor immediately so that appropriate care can be given.

In addition to these positions, other cardiovascular technologists specialize in a particular aspect of health care. For example, *cardiopulmonary technologists* specialize in procedures for diagnosing problems with the heart and lungs. They may conduct electrocardiograph, phonocardiograph (sound recordings of the heart's valves and of the blood passing through them), echocardiograph, stress testing, and respiratory test procedures.

Cardiopulmonary technologists also may assist on cardiac catheterization procedures, measuring and recording information about the patient's cardiovascular and pulmonary systems during the procedure and alerting the cardiac catheterization team to any problems.

REQUIREMENTS

High School

At a minimum, cardiovascular technologists need a high school diploma or equivalent to enter the field. Although no specific high school classes will directly prepare you to be a technologist, good study skills and a firm grounding in basic high school subjects are important to all technologist positions.

During high school, you should take English, health, biology, and typing. You also might consider courses in social sciences to help you understand the social and psychological needs of patients.

Postsecondary Training

In the past, many EKG operators were trained on the job by an EKG supervisor. This still may be true for some EKG technician positions. Increasingly, however, EKG technologists get postsecondary schooling before they are hired. Holter monitoring and stress testing may be part of your EKG schooling, or they may be learned through additional training. Ultrasound and cardiology technologists tend to have the most postsecondary schooling (up to a four-year bachelor's degree) and have the most extensive academic/experience requirements for credentialing purposes.

You can enter these positions without having had previous health care experience. However, some previous exposure to the business side of health care or even training in related areas is helpful. With academic training or professional experience in nursing, radiology science, or respiratory science, for example, you may be able to move into cardiology technology.

As a rule of thumb, medical employers value postsecondary schooling that gives you actual hands-on experience with patients in addition to classroom training. At many of the schools that train cardiovascular technologists, you work with patients in a variety of health care settings and train on more than one brand of equipment.

Some employers still have a physician or EKG department manager train EKG technicians on the job. Training generally lasts from one to six months. Trainees learn how to operate the EKG machine, how to produce and edit the electrocardiogram, and other related tasks.

Some vocational, technical, and junior colleges have one- or two-year training programs in EKG technology, Holter monitoring, stress testing, or all three; otherwise, EKG technologists may obtain training in Holter and stress procedures after they've already started working, either on the job or through an additional six months or more of schooling. Formal academic programs give technologists more preparation in the subject than is available with most on-the-job training and allow them to earn a certificate (one-year programs) or associate's degree (two-year programs). The American Medical Association (AMA)'s *Allied Health Directory* has listings of accredited EKG programs.

Ultrasound technologists usually need a high school diploma or equivalent plus one, two, or four years of postsecondary schooling in a trade school, technical school, or community college. Vascular technologists also may be trained on the job. Again, a list of accredited programs can be found in the AMA's *Allied Health Directory;* also, a directory of training opportunities in sonography is available from the Society of Diagnostic Medical Sonography.

Cardiology technologists tend to have the highest academic requirements of all: a four-year bachelor of science degree, a two-year associate's degree, or a certificate of completion from a hospital, trade, or technical cardiovascular program. A two-year program at a junior or community college might include one year of core classes (e.g., mathematics, biology, chemistry, and anatomy) and one year of specialized classes in cardiology procedures.

Cardiac monitor technicians need a high school diploma or equivalent, with additional educational requirements similar to those of EKG technicians.

Certification or Licensing

Right now, certification or licensing for cardiovascular technologists is voluntary, but the move to state licensing is expected in the near future. Many credentialing bodies for cardiovascular and pulmonary positions exist, including American Registry of Diagnostic Medical Sonographers (ARDMS), Cardiovascular Credentialing International (CCI), and others, and there are more than a dozen possible credentials for cardiovascular technologists. For example, sonographers can take an exam from ARDMS to receive credentialing in sonography. Their credentials may be as registered diagnostic medical sonographer, registered diagnostic cardiac sonographer, or registered vascular technologist. Credentialing requirements for cardiology technologists or ultrasound technologists may include a test plus formal academic and on-the-job requirements. Professional experience or academic training in a related field, such as nursing, radiology science, and respiratory science, may be acceptable as part of these formal academic and professional requirements. As with continuing education, certification is a sign of interest and dedication to the field and is generally favorably regarded by potential employers.

Cardiology is a cutting-edge area of medicine that undergoes constant advancements, and medical equipment relating to the heart is

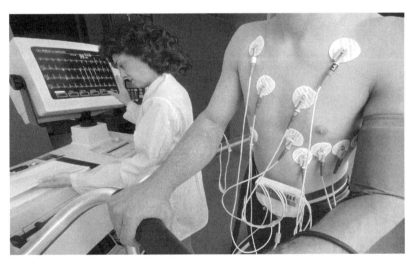

A cardiovascular technician administers a stress test. (*Corbis*)

continually updated. Therefore, keeping up with new developments is vital. In addition, technologists who add to their qualifications through taking part in continuing education tend to earn more money and have more employment opportunities. Major professional societies encourage and provide the opportunities for professionals to continue their education.

Other Requirements

Technicians must be able to put patients at ease about the procedure they are to undergo. Therefore, you should be pleasant, patient, alert, and able to understand and sympathize with the feelings of others. When explaining a procedure to patients, cardiovascular technicians should be able to do so in a calm, reassuring, and confident manner.

EXPLORING

Prospective cardiovascular technologists will find it difficult to gain any direct experience on a part-time basis in electrocardiography. The first experience with the work generally comes during on-the-job training sessions. You may, however, be able to gain some exposure to patient-care activities in general by signing up for volunteer work at a local hospital. In addition, you can arrange to visit a hospital, clinic, or physician's office where electrocardiographs are taken. In this way, you may be able to watch a technician at work or at least talk to a technician about what the work is like.

EMPLOYERS

There are approximately 39,000 cardiovascular technologists employed in the United States. Most work in hospitals, but employment can be found in physicians' offices, clinics, rehab centers, or anyplace electrocardiographs are taken.

STARTING OUT

Because most cardiovascular technologists receive their initial training on their first job, great care should be taken in finding your first employer. Pay close attention not only to the pay and working conditions, but also to the kind of on-the-job training that is provided for each prospective position. High school vocational counselors may be able to tell you which hospitals have good reputations for EKG training programs. Applying directly to hospitals is a common way of entering the field. Information also can be gained by reading the classified ads in the newspaper and from talking with friends and relatives who work in hospitals.

For students who graduate from one- to two-year training programs, finding a first job should be easier. First, employers are always eager to hire people who are already trained. Second, these graduates can be less concerned about the training programs offered by their employers. Third, they should find that their teachers and guidance counselors can be excellent sources of information about job possibilities in the area. If the training program includes practical experience, graduates may find that the hospital in which they trained or worked before graduation would be willing to hire them after graduation.

ADVANCEMENT

Opportunities for advancement are best for cardiovascular technologists who learn to do or assist with more complex procedures, such as stress testing, Holter monitoring, echocardiography, and cardiac catheterization. With proper training and experience, these technicians may eventually become cardiovascular technologists, echocardiography technologists, cardiopulmonary technicians, cardiology technologists, or other specialty technicians or technologists.

In addition to these kinds of specialty positions, experienced technicians may also be able to advance to various supervisory and training posts.

EARNINGS

The median salary for cardiovascular technologists was $33,350 in 2000, according to the U.S. Department of Labor. The lowest paid 10 percent earned less than $19,540, and the highest paid 10 percent earned more than $52,930 annually. Earnings can vary by size and type of employer. For example, technologists working in physicians' offices had the median annual income $33,100, while those in hospitals had the median $32,860. Those with formal training earn more than those who trained on the job, and those who are able to perform more sophisticated tests, such as Holter monitoring and stress testing, are paid more than those who perform only the basic electrocardiograph tests.

Technologists working in hospitals receive the same fringe benefits as other hospital workers, including medical insurance, paid vacations, and sick leave. In some cases, benefits also include educational assistance, retirement plans, and uniform allowances.

WORK ENVIRONMENT

Cardiovascular technologists usually work in clean, quiet, well-lighted surroundings. They generally work five-day, 40-hour weeks, although technicians working in small hospitals may be on 24-hour call for emergencies, and all technicians in hospitals, large or small, can expect to do occasional evening or weekend work. With the growing emphasis on cost containment in health care, more jobs are likely to develop in outpatient settings, so in the future it is likely that cardiovascular technologists will work more often in clinics, health maintenance organizations, and other nonhospital locations.

Cardiovascular technologists generally work with patients who are ill or who have reason to fear they might be ill. With this in mind, there are opportunities for the technicians to do these people some good, but there is also a chance of causing some unintentional harm as well: A well-conducted test can reduce anxieties or make a physician's job easier; a misplaced electrode or an error in recordkeeping could cause an incorrect diagnosis. Technicians need to be able to cope with these responsibilities and consistently conduct their work in the best interests of their patients.

Part of the technician's job includes putting patients at ease about the procedure they are to undergo. Toward that end, technicians should be pleasant, patient, alert, and able to understand and sympathize with the feelings of others. In explaining the nature of the procedure to patients, cardiovascular technicians should be able to do so in a calm, reassuring, and confident manner.

Inevitably, some patients will try to get information about their medical situation from the technician. Technicians must remind patients that the interpretation is for the physician to make.

Another large part of a technician's job involves getting along well with other members of the hospital staff. This task is sometimes made more difficult by the fact that in most hospitals there is a formal, often rigid, status structure, and cardiovascular technologists may find themselves in a relatively low position in that structure. In emergency situations or at other moments of frustration, cardiovascular technologists may find themselves dealt with brusquely or angrily. Technicians should not take outbursts or rude treatment personally, but instead should respond with stability and maturity.

OUTLOOK

The overall employment of cardiovascular technologists and technicians should grow faster than the average through 2010, according to the U.S. Department of Labor. Growth will be primarily due to the increasing numbers of older people who have a higher incidence of heart problems. However, the Department of Labor projects employment for EKG technicians to decline during this same period as hospitals train other health care personnel to perform basic EKG procedures.

FOR MORE INFORMATION

For information on careers, contact
Alliance of Cardiovascular Professionals
4456 Corporation Lane, #164
Virginia Beach, VA 23462
Tel: 757-497-1225
http://www.acp-online.org

For information on the medical field, including listings of accredited medical programs, contact
American Medical Association
515 North State Street
Chicago, IL 60610
Tel: 312-464-5000
http://www.ama-assn.org

For information on certification or licensing, contact
American Registry of Diagnostic Medical Sonographers
51 Monroe Street
Plaza East One
Rockville, MD 20850-2400
Tel: 800-541-9754
http://www.ardms.org

For information on credentials, contact
Cardiovascular Credentialing International
4456 Corporation Lane, Suite 120
Virginia Beach, VA 23462
Tel: 800-326-0268
http://cci-online.org

Dental Laboratory Technicians

OVERVIEW

Dental laboratory technicians are skilled craftspeople who make and repair dental appliances, such as dentures, inlays, bridges, crowns, and braces, according to dentists' written prescriptions. They work with plastics, ceramics, and metals, using models of a patient's mouth or teeth made from impressions taken by the dentist. Some dental laboratory technicians, especially those who work for smaller dental laboratories, perform a whole range of laboratory activities, while many others specialize in only one area. Some specialties include making orthodontic appliances, such as braces for straightening teeth; applying layers of porcelain paste or acrylic resin over a metal framework to form crowns, bridges, and tooth facings; making and repairing wire frames and retainers for teeth used in partial dentures; and making and repairing full and partial dentures. Job titles often reflect a specialization. For example, technicians who make porcelain restorations are dental ceramicists. There are approximately 43,000 dental laboratory technicians of all types working in the United States.

HISTORY

Dental laboratory technicians are little known to most people who visit dentists, yet many dental patients today benefit from their skills. For centuries people have used many kinds of false teeth, with varying success. Thanks to sophisticated techniques and new materials, such as acrylics and plastics, there are efficient, comfortable, and cosmetically acceptable aids available when natural teeth or tissue are missing or unsatisfactory.

Today nearly all dental practitioners utilize the services provided by commercial dental laboratories that handle tasks for a number of practitioners. This was not always the case, however.

Until the last years of the 19th century, dentists performed all their own lab work. The first successful commercial dental laboratory was established in 1887 by a partnership of a dentist and a machinist. The idea of delegating work to such laboratories was slow to catch on before World War II, when many dental technicians were trained to provide services at scattered military bases and on ships. In 1940 there were about 2,700 commercial dental laboratories in the United States; there are several times that number today. Their average size has remained small—only about half a dozen full-time workers per laboratory. A growing number of technicians are employed directly by dentists, most notably specialists in prosthodontics and orthodontics, to staff private dental laboratories.

At first, dental laboratory technicians were trained on the job, but formal training programs are now the best way to prepare. In 1951, the American Dental Association began to accredit two-year postsecondary programs in dental technology. Currently there are just over 30 accredited institutions offering such training.

THE JOB

Dental laboratory technicians often find that their talents and preferences lead them toward one particular type of work in their field. The broad areas of specialization open to them include full and partial dentures, crowns and bridges, ceramics, and orthodontics.

Complete dentures, also called false teeth or plates, are worn by people who have had all their teeth removed from the upper or lower jaw, or from both jaws. *Denture specialists* apply their knowledge of oral anatomy and restoration to carefully position teeth in a wax model for the best occlusion (how the upper and lower teeth fit together when the mouth is closed) and then build up wax over the denture model. After the denture is cast in place, they clean and buff the product, using a bench lathe equipped with polishing wheels. When repairing dentures, they may cast plaster models of replacement parts and match the new tooth's color and shape to the natural or adjacent teeth. They cast reproductions of gums, fill cracks in dentures, and rebuild linings using acrylics and plastics. They may also bend and solder wire made of gold, platinum, and other metals and sometimes fabricate wire using a centrifugal casting machine.

Removable partial dentures, often called partials, restore missing teeth for patients who have some teeth remaining on the jaw. The materials and techniques used to manufacture partials are similar to those for full dentures. In addition, wire clasps are mounted to anchor the partial denture to the remaining teeth yet allow it to be removed for cleaning. Fixed partial dentures serve the same purpose as removable ones, but are cemented to the adjacent teeth rather than anchored by clasps.

Crown and bridge specialists restore the missing parts of a natural tooth to recreate it in its original form. Fixed partial dentures, made of plastics and metal, are sometimes called fixed bridgework because they are permanently cemented to the natural part of the tooth and are not removable. A crown is permanently cemented to a single tooth. Technicians in this area are skilled at melting and casting metals. Waxing (building up wax around the setup before casting) and polishing the finished appliance are also among crown and bridge specialists' responsibilities.

Some dental laboratory technicians are porcelain specialists and are known as *dental ceramicists*. They fabricate natural-looking replacements to fit over natural teeth or to replace missing ones. Many patients concerned with personal appearance seek porcelain crowns, especially on front teeth. The ability to match color exactly and delicately shape teeth is crucial for these technicians. To create crowns, bridges, and tooth facings (veneers), dental ceramicists apply multiple layers of mineral powders to a metal base and fuse the materials in an oven. The process is repeated until the result conforms exactly to specifications. Ceramicists must know and understand all phases of dental technology and possess natural creative abilities. Because they require the highest level of knowledge and talent, ceramicists are generally the best paid of dental technicians.

Orthodontics, the final area of specialization for dental laboratory technicians, involves bending wire into intricate shapes and soldering wires into complex positions. *Orthodontic technicians* shape, grind, polish, carve, and assemble metal and plastic appliances. Although tooth-straightening devices such as retainers, positioners, and tooth bands are not considered permanent, they may have to stay in place for several years.

Dental laboratory technicians may work in a general or full-service laboratory, a category that includes nearly half of all dental laboratories. Or they may find employment with a laboratory that performs specialized services. Most specialized laboratories are concerned with the various uses of a particular material. For example, one specializing in acrylics is likely to make complete and partial dentures; another laboratory that does gold work will make gold inlays and bridges.

Did You Know?

Dentures, or "false teeth," as they are commonly known, are believed to have been invented by the Etruscans more than 2,000 years ago, when that society's remedy for tooth decay—rinsing the mouth with wine that had been boiled with dog teeth—proved less than effective.

For several centuries, dentures were made from materials such as hippopotamus or whale ivory and were not custom-fitted as they are today, thus making them very painful to wear. Despite this, in societies such as ancient Greece and Rome, dentures were seen as prestigious status symbols, as only the very wealthy could afford this luxury item.

As a result of the many advances in dental laboratory technology that occurred in the 20th century, dentures are now made from complex plastics and are fitted to a patient's mouth to look and feel as natural as possible.

Source: South-African Dental Association, http://www.sadnet.co.za

The lab's size may be related to the kinds of tasks its technical employees perform. Some large commercial laboratories may have staffs of 50 or more, allowing for a high degree of specialization. On the other hand, technicians working in a one- or two-person private laboratory may be called on to do a wide range of jobs.

REQUIREMENTS

High School

Your must have a high school diploma to become a dental laboratory technician. Useful high school courses include biology, chemistry, shop (wood or metal working), mechanical drawing, art, and ceramics. Any other course or activity that allows you to learn about metallurgy or the chemistry of plastics would be very helpful.

Postsecondary Training

Although there is a growing trend among technicians to get an associate's degree, most technicians today still enter the field by completing three to four years of on-the-job training. These technicians work as trainees under the supervision of experienced technicians in a dental laboratory. Trainees start by doing simple jobs, such as mixing plaster and pouring it into molds. As they gradually gain experience, they are assigned more complex tasks.

Increasing numbers of technicians enroll in a formal training program that leads to an associate's degree in applied science. There are currently about 35 training programs in the United States, including military programs. A typical two-year curriculum might include courses in denture construction, processing and repairing dentures, tooth construction, waxing and casting inlays, and constructing crowns. In addition, the student may be expected to take courses such as biochemistry, English, business mathematics, and American government.

Although newly graduated technicians still need several years of work experience to refine their practical skills, these graduates benefit from a program combining academic courses with laboratory instruction. Exposure to a wide range of skills and materials pays off in the long run for most graduates. Employers often prefer to hire new employees with this type of formal academic training.

Certification or Licensing

Technicians with appropriate training and experience can become certified dental technicians, thus earning the right to place the initials CDT after their names. Certification is conducted by the National Board for Certification in Dental Laboratory Technology. For initial certification, candidates must pass a basic written and practical examination in at least one of the five laboratory specialties: complete dentures, partial dentures, crowns and bridges, ceramics, and orthodontics.

Certification requirements also include two years of professional experience for those who have completed an accredited associate's degree program. Those who have become technicians through on-the-job training need to have five years of work experience in the field. Every year certified dental technicians must meet specific continuing education requirements in order to maintain certification status. Although certification is not mandatory for employment, many employers regard it as the best evidence of competence.

Other Requirements

Although membership is not required, dental laboratory technicians may choose to belong to various professional organizations. The most prominent among these are the National Association of Dental Laboratories and the American Dental Association. Local meetings bring together technicians and laboratory owners to share ideas of common interest and information about job opportunities.

Successful dental laboratory technicians possess the precision, patience, and dexterity of a skilled artisan. They must be able to carry out written and sometimes verbal instructions to the letter because each dental fixture has to be constructed according to very specific designs provided by the dentist. Good eyesight and good color discrimination, as well as the ability to do delicate work with one's fingers, are very important. Although it is by no means a requirement, prospective dental laboratory technicians will profit from experience building model airplanes or cars, and other such work that involves mixing and molding various materials.

EXPLORING

High school students with an interest in dental laboratory technology can seek out courses and activities that allow exploration of ceramics, metal casting and soldering, molding, and the related skills practiced by dental laboratory technicians. In addition, a local dentist or school guidance counselor may be able to recommend a technician or laboratory in the area that the student might visit in order to get a firsthand idea of the work involved.

Part-time or summer jobs as laboratory helpers may be available to high school students. Such positions usually consist of picking up and delivering work to dentists' offices, but they may also provide a chance for the student to observe and assist practicing dental laboratory technicians. Students in dental laboratory technology training programs often have part-time jobs that develop into full-time technician positions upon graduation.

Interested students may also call their state dental laboratory association or a local commercial laboratory to find out when seminars and lectures are held. By attending such events, a student can learn more about dental laboratory issues and techniques and can also talk with laboratory technicians.

EMPLOYERS

The majority of technicians work in commercial dental laboratories. Thousands of dental laboratories are located throughout the United States. Some of these laboratories are small, with only one or two technicians who perform a broad range of duties. Large commercial laboratories that serve dentists from a wider area or accept work through the mail may employ from two to 200 technicians; in such laboratories, technicians are more likely to specialize in one area. Some opportunities are available for technicians in private dental offices, dental schools, hospitals, and companies that manufacture dental prosthetic materials. Experienced technicians may find teaching positions in dental laboratory technology education programs.

The military provides dental care to members of the armed forces and their dependents. The branches of the armed forces train laboratory technicians and have their own laboratories that employ technicians who are serving in the military.

Experienced technicians may choose to establish their own laboratories. Thus, some laboratory technicians are self-employed.

STARTING OUT

Newly graduated dental laboratory technicians seeking employment can apply directly to laboratories and dentists' offices as well as to private and state employment agencies. The best way to locate vacancies is through school placement offices.

Local chapters of professional associations are a good way to make contacts and keep up with new developments and employment openings. Sometimes more experienced dental technicians can get leads by inquiring at dental supply houses. Their sales workers are in constant contact with dentists and laboratories in the area and often know something about staffing needs.

In general, entry-level jobs are likely to include training and routine tasks that allow the technician to become familiar with the laboratory's operations. In a very large commercial laboratory, for instance, newcomers may be assigned to various departments. At the plaster bench they may make and trim models; some technicians may do routine minor repairs of dentures and other appliances; others may polish dentures. As their skills develop, beginning dental laboratory technicians gradually take on more complicated tasks.

The armed forces also provide dental laboratory technology training to enlistees who will work in the military's dental laboratories.

ADVANCEMENT

The best way to advance is to develop individual skills. Technicians can expect advancement as they become expert in a specialized type of work. Depending on skill, experience, and education, some technicians become supervisors or managers in commercial laboratories. Such promotions often depend on the employee having an associate's degree, so many technicians who began their careers with on-the-job training eventually return for formal education.

Technicians interested in advancing can find out about new methods and update their skills in many ways. Professional organizations provide a variety of learning opportunities. Materials manufacturers also offer courses, often free of charge, in the use of their products; outstanding technicians may be hired as instructors in these courses.

Some dental laboratory technicians, seeking variety and new outlets for their creativity, develop sideline activities that require similar skills and materials. Fine jewelry making, for example, is a natural career development for some technicians. Some technicians become teachers in training programs; others become sales representatives for dental products manufacturers.

Many technicians aspire to own and operate an independent laboratory. This requires a broad understanding of dental laboratory work, a well-developed business sense, and a considerable investment. Nonetheless, most of today's commercial laboratory owners have worked as laboratory technicians themselves.

EARNINGS

Dental laboratory trainees earn slightly more than minimum wage. As technicians gain experience, however, their salaries increase. The U.S. Department of Labor reported that in 2000 the median yearly income for dental laboratory technicians was about $26,915. The department also reported that the lowest paid 10 percent of this group earned roughly $16,182 per year, while the highest paid 10 percent earned about $44,657 annually. Median hourly earnings of dental laboratory technicians in 2000 were $12.88 in offices and clinics of dentists and $12.87 in medical and dental laboratories. According to the National Association of Dental Laboratories, an especially productive or skilled technician may earn as much as $60,000. Self-employed technicians and those who work in smaller laboratories and perform a variety of work exceed the average earnings.

Benefits vary by individual laboratories. Additional benefits available to members of the National Association of Dental Laboratories include major medical and surgical insurance, term life insurance, dental insurance, and disability income coverage.

WORK ENVIRONMENT

Most dental laboratory technicians work in well-lighted, calm, and pleasant surroundings. Technicians usually have their own workbenches and equipment. Because some pieces of equipment produce high levels of noise, dental laboratory technicians may wish to have their hearing checked periodically.

The normal workweek for technicians employed in commercial laboratories is 40 hours. Sometimes technicians face deadline pressure, although dentists' requirements are usually flexible enough to allow for special problems or difficult jobs. Many laboratories must operate on weekends, and in areas where there is a shortage of technicians, it may be necessary to work overtime, with wages adjusted accordingly. Self-employed technicians or those in very small laboratories may have irregular or longer hours.

Technicians usually work by themselves, concentrating on details of the pieces they are making or repairing. While the work does not demand great physical strength, it does require deft handling of materials and tools. Technicians usually have little contact with people other than their immediate coworkers and the dentists whose instructions they follow. Work is often brought in and out by messengers or by mail.

Successful dental laboratory technicians enjoy detailed work, are good at following instructions, and take pride in perfection. They should enjoy working independently but still be able to coordinate their activities with other workers in the same laboratory when necessary.

OUTLOOK

Although the overall demand for dental laboratory technicians is expected to grow more slowly than the average through 2010, certain job opportunities will remain favorable, according to the U.S. Department of Labor. Trainee positions may be readily available, but such positions offer relatively low entry-level salaries. Experienced technicians with established professional reputations can start their own laboratories to advance their careers.

The slowing demand for dental laboratory technicians is related to the success of preventive dentistry. Because they are more likely to keep their own teeth, fewer dental patients will need complete dentures. More patients will need partial dentures or crowns, however, which also require laboratory work. As the baby boomer generation ages, they may require more dental care.

The reduced demand for dental laboratory work may be partly offset by increased demand for tooth-colored fillings to replace silver amalgam fillings. Although health problems related to the mercury in amalgam fillings are rare, some patients opt for replacement. Also, the affluent baby boomer generation is often willing to pay for more costly cosmetic restorations, such as all-ceramic crowns and dental implants.

FOR MORE INFORMATION

The ADA promotes dental health and the dental profession through education, research, and advocacy; publishes the Journal of the American Dental Association *and ADA News; and holds an annual conference. For more information, contact*
American Dental Association (ADA)
Department of Career Guidance
211 East Chicago Avenue

Chicago, IL 60611
Tel: 312-440-2500
Email: publicinfo@ada.org
http://www.ada.org

For information on publications, conferences, and certification, contact
National Association of Dental Laboratories
1530 Metropolitan Boulevard
Tallahassee, FL 32308
Tel: 800-950-1150
Email: nadl@nadl.org
http://www.nadl.org

Diagnostic Medical Sonographers

OVERVIEW

Diagnostic medical sonographers, or *sonographers,* use advanced technology in the form of high-frequency sound waves similar to sonar to produce two-dimensional, gray-scale images of the internal body for analysis by radiologists and other physicians. There are about 33,000 diagnostic medical sonographers employed in the United States.

HISTORY

Pierre Curie discovered a procedure to produce ultrasonic vibrations in 1890. It was not until World War II, however, that ultrasound gained a practical application in the form of SONAR, an ultrasonic device used to detect submarines beneath water. In the 1960s, ultrasound gained a medical use. The medical industry sought a safer and more effective way of imaging fetuses. Ultrasound provided the answer: the echoes created by ultrasonic sound waves gave physicians and obstetricians a safe way to monitor the development of the fetus.

Ultrasound technology has since been adapted for other medical uses, including the heating of deep tissue to treat such ailments as arthritis and bursitis, and in bloodless brain surgery. Dentists also use ultrasound to remove calcium deposits from the surface of teeth. In addition to its medical uses, ultrasound is used in the plastics, precious metal and gemstone, electronic, textile, and welding industries.

THE JOB

Sonographers work on the orders of a physician or radiologist. They are responsible for the proper set up and selection of the ultrasound equipment for each specific exam. They explain the procedure to patients, recording any additional information that may be of later use to the physician. Sonographers instruct patients and assist them into the proper physical position so that the test may begin.

When the patient is properly aligned, the sonographer applies a gel to the skin that improves the diagnostic image. The sonographer selects the transducer, a microphone-shaped device that directs high-frequency sound waves into the area to be imaged, and adjusts equipment controls according to the proper depth of field and specific organ or structure to be examined. The transducer is moved as the sonographer monitors the sound-wave display screen in order to ensure that a quality ultrasonic image is being produced. Sonographers must master the location and visualization of human anatomy to be able to differentiate clearly between healthy and pathological areas.

When a clear image is obtained, the sonographer activates equipment that records individual photographic views or sequences as real-time images of the affected area. These images are recorded on computer disk, magnetic tape, strip printout, film, or videotape. The sonographer removes the film after recording and prepares it for analysis by the physician. In order to be able to discuss the procedure

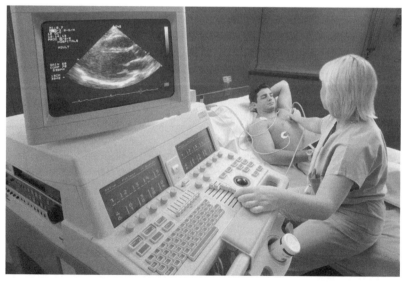

Diagnostic medical sonographers must strike a balance between professionalism and empathy while conducting procedures. (*Corbis*)

with the physician, if asked, the sonographer may also record any further data or observations that occurred during the exam.

Other duties include updating patient records, monitoring and adjusting sonographic equipment to maintain accuracy, and, after considerable experience, preparing work schedules and evaluating potential equipment purchases.

REQUIREMENTS

High School

If you are interested in a career in sonography, in high school you should take courses in mathematics, biology, physics, anatomy and physiology, and, especially, chemistry. Also, take English and speech classes to improve your communication skills. In this career you will be working with both patients and other medical professionals, and it will be important for you to be able to follow directions as well as explain procedures. Finally, take computer courses to familiarize yourself with using technology.

Postsecondary Training

Instruction in diagnostic medical sonography is offered by hospitals, colleges, universities, technical schools, and the armed forces in the form of hospital certificates, and two-year associate's and four-year bachelor's degree programs. Most sonographers enter the field after completing an associate's degree. The Joint Review Committee on Education in Diagnostic Medical Sonography (a division of the Commission on Accreditation of Allied Health Education Programs) has accredited more than 70 programs in the United States. Education consists of classroom and laboratory instruction, as well as hands-on experience in the form of internships in a hospital ultrasound department. Areas of study include patient care and medical ethics, general and cross-sectional anatomy, physiology and pathophysiology, applications and limitations of ultrasound, and image evaluation.

Certification or Licensing

After completing their degrees, sonographers may register with the American Registry of Diagnostic Medical Sonographers (ARDMS). Registration allows qualified sonographers to take the National Boards to gain certification, which, although optional, is frequently required by employers. Other licensing requirements may exist at the state level but vary greatly.

Students should also be aware of continuing education requirements that exist to keep sonographers at the forefront of current technology and diagnostic theory. They are required to maintain certification through continuing education classes, which vary from state to state. This continuing education, offered by hospitals and ultrasound equipment companies, is usually offered after regular work hours have ended.

Other Requirements

On a personal level, prospective sonographers need to be technically adept, detail-oriented, and precision minded. You need to enjoy helping others and working with a variety of professionals as part of a team. You must be able to follow physician instructions, while maintaining a creative approach to imaging as you complete each procedure. Sonographers need to cultivate a professional demeanor, while still expressing empathy, patience, and understanding in order to reassure patients. This professionalism is also necessary because tragedies such as cancer, untreatable disease, or fetal death are revealed during imaging procedures. As a result, sonographers must be able to skillfully deflect questions better left to the radiologist or the attending physician. Clear communication, both verbal and written, is a plus for those who are part of a health care team.

EXPLORING

Although you can only gain direct experience in sonography through proper education and certification, you can gain insight into duties and responsibilities by speaking directly to an experienced sonographer. You can visit a hospital, health maintenance organization, or other locations to view the equipment and facilities used and to watch professionals at work. You may also consider contacting teachers at schools of diagnostic medical sonography or touring their educational facilities. Guidance counselors or science teachers may also be able to arrange a presentation by a sonographer.

EMPLOYERS

While hospitals are the main employers of sonographers, increasing employment opportunities exist in nursing homes, HMOs, imaging centers, private physicians' offices, research laboratories, educational institutions, and industry.

STARTING OUT

Those interested in becoming diagnostic medical sonographers must complete a sonographic educational program such as one offered by teaching hospitals, colleges and universities, technical schools, and the armed forces. You should be sure to enroll in an accredited educational program, as those who complete such a program stand the best chances for employment.

Voluntary registration with the American Registry of Diagnostic Medical Sonographers (ARDMS) is key to gaining employment. Most employers require registration with ARDMS. Other methods of entering the field include responding to job listings in sonography publications, registering with employment agencies specializing in the health care field, contacting headhunters, or applying to the personnel offices of health care employers.

ADVANCEMENT

Many advancement areas are open to sonographers who have considerable experience and, more importantly, advanced education. Sonographers with a bachelor's degree stand the best chance to gain additional duties or responsibilities. Technical programs, teaching hospitals, colleges, universities, and, sometimes, in-house training programs can provide this further training. Highly trained and experienced sonographers can rise to the position of chief technologist, administrator, or clinical supervisor, overseeing sonography departments, choosing new equipment, and creating work schedules. Others may become sonography instructors, teaching ultrasound technology in hospitals, universities, and other educational settings. Other sonographers may gravitate toward marketing, working as ultrasound equipment sales representatives and selling ultrasound technology to medical clients. Sonographers involved in sales may market ultrasound technology for nonmedical uses to the plastics, steel, or other industries. Sonographers may also work as machinery demonstrators, traveling at the behest of manufacturers to train others in the use of new or updated equipment.

Sonographers may pursue advanced education in conjunction with or in addition to their sonography training. Sonographers may become certified in computer tomography, magnetic resonance imaging, nuclear medicine technology, radiation therapy, and cardiac catheterization. Others may become diagnostic cardiac sonographers or focus on specialty areas such as obstetrics/gynecology, neurosonography, peripheral vascular doppler, and ophthalmology.

EARNINGS

According to the U.S. Department of Labor, diagnostic medical sonographers earned a median annual income of $44,820 in 2000. The lowest paid 10 percent of this group, which included those just begin-ning in the field, made approximately $32,470. The highest paid 10 percent, which included those with experience and managerial duties, earned more than $59,310 annually. Median earnings for those who worked in hospitals were $43,950 and for those employed in offices and clinics of medical doctors, $46,190.

Pay scales vary based on experience, educational level, and type and location of employer, with urban employers offering higher com-pensation than rural areas and small towns. Beyond base salaries, sonographers can expect to enjoy many fringe benefits, including paid vacation, sick and personal days, and health and dental insurance.

WORK ENVIRONMENT

A variety of work settings exist for sonographers, from health main-tenance organizations to mobile imaging centers to clinical research labs or industry. In health care settings, diagnostic medical sonogra-phers may work in departments of obstetrics/gynecology, cardiology, neurology, and others.

Sonographers enjoy an indoor workplace that is clean, well light-ed, quiet, and professional. Most sonographers work at one location, although mobile imaging sonographers and sales representatives can expect a considerable amount of travel.

The typical sonographer is constantly busy, seeing as many as 25 patients in the course of an eight-hour day. Some employers may also require overtime. The types of examinations vary by institution, but common areas include fetal ultrasounds, gynecological (i.e., uterus, ovaries), and abdominal (i.e., gallbladder, liver, and kidney) tests. Prospective sonographers should be aware of the occasionally repet-itive nature of the job and the long hours usually spent standing. Daily duties may be both physically and mentally taxing. Although they are not exposed to harmful radiation, sonographers may nevertheless be exposed to communicable diseases and hazardous materials from invasive procedures. Universal safety standards exist to ensure sono-graphers' safety.

OUTLOOK

According to the U.S. Department of Labor, employment of diagnos-tic medical sonographers should grow faster than the average through 2010. One reason for this growth is that sonography is a safe, nonra-dioactive imaging process. In addition, sonography has proved suc-cessful in detecting life-threatening diseases and in analyzing previously nonimageable internal organs. Sonography will play an increasing role in the fields of obstetrics/gynecology and cardiology. Furthermore, the aging population will create high demand for qualified technologists to operate diagnostic machinery. Demand for qualified diagnostic medical sonographers exceeds the current supply in some areas of the country, especially rural communities, small towns, and some retirement areas. Being flexible about location and compensation will lead to the best opportunities in current and future job markets.

A few important factors may slow growth. The health care industry is currently in a state of transition because of public and government debate concerning Medicare, universal health care, and the role of third-party payers in the system. Also, some procedures may prove too costly for insurance companies or government programs to cover. Hospital sonography departments will also be affected by this debate and continue to downsize. Some procedures will be done only on weekends, weeknights, or on an outpatient basis, possibly affecting employment opportunities, hours, and salaries of future sonographers. Conversely, nursing homes, HMOs, mobile imaging centers, and private physicians' groups will offer new employment opportunities to highly skilled sonographers.

Anyone considering a career in sonography should be aware that there is considerable competition for the most lucrative jobs. Those flexible in regard to hours, salary, and location and who possess advanced education stand to prosper in future job markets. Those complementing their sonographic skills with training in other imaging areas, such as magnetic resonance imaging, computer tomography, nuclear medicine technology, or other specialties, will best be able to meet the changing requirements and rising competition of future job markets.

FOR MORE INFORMATION

For information about available jobs and credentials, contact
American Registry of Diagnostic Medical Sonographers
51 Monroe Street, Plaza East One
Rockville, MD 20850-2400
Tel: 800-541-9754
http://www.ardms.org

For information regarding accredited programs of sonography, contact
Commission on Accreditation of Allied Health Education
    Programs
35 East Wacker Drive, Suite 1970
Chicago, IL 60601-2208
Tel: 312-553-9355

Email: caahep@caahep.org
http://www.caahep.org

For information regarding a career in sonography or to subscribe to the Journal of Diagnostic Medical Sonography, *contact*
Society of Diagnostic Medical Sonography
2745 Dallas Parkway, Suite 350
Plano, TX 75093-4706
Tel: 800-229-9506
http://www.sdms.org

———————————— **INTERVIEW** ————————————

Anne Conner-Day has been working in diagnostic medical sonography for more than 25 years. She is a co-owner of the Sonography Education Academy in North Carolina and serves as an educational consultant for sonography programs at several institutions. She spoke with the editors of Careers in Focus: Medical Technicians *about her career and the field of diagnostic medical sonography.*

Q. Please describe the responsibilities of your job.

A. I provide distance education opportunities to underserved populations to help them enter the profession of diagnostic medical sonography. This is a new area and a new company, which is just now getting off the ground. I also consult with several universities and medical centers in curriculum development and online education.

I currently work out of my home, although clinical site visitation will occur in the future. When I am consulting, I attend various meetings both online and in person. I also serve as a regional director for the Society of Diagnostic Medical Sonography and spend part of my day in this voluntary activity promoting medical sonography to the public and assisting our membership.

Q. What were your expectations entering this field? Are they much different from the realities?

A. In the mid-1970s, when I entered this field, I was fascinated by the prospects in diagnostic medical sonography. I enjoyed the personal contact with patients and the eye-hand coordination required of a sonographer. I also enjoyed the correlation of anatomy to pathological conditions and the responsibility placed on the sonographer to help in the final diagnosis. In the past 25 years I have seen the profession grow tremendously with imaging capabilities far surpassing early expectations of equipment and diagnostic abilities.

One negative result of years of scanning patients is the high rate of musculoskeletal disorders that occur in sonographers due to their scanning techniques and equipment. These issues are currently being dealt with by hospitals and medical centers, which are purchasing the proper equipment needed for sonographers to avoid muscular strain injuries. Current education of student sonographers involves learning methods and techniques that will help prevent musculoskeletal injuries in people entering the profession.

Q. What kind of education and training did you pursue for this position?

A. I began my health career as a radiologic technologist. In the 1970s these were the typical people who entered the profession of sonography. However, sonographers now can be successfully educated without this background; people from many different professions are entering the field, as well as graduates of associate degree programs in community colleges and bachelor degree programs in universities. It is important for someone wishing to enter this profession to look for a CAAHEP-accredited program, which will ensure minimum standards are being met.

When I chose to enter the field of education I received a bachelor's degree in medical imaging and a master's degree in health care administration.

Q. Did you complete any internships or clinical practice to help you prepare for your career?

A. I was required to scan for one year prior to taking certification examinations in the late 1970s and early 1980s. However, a minimum of 18 months of scanning is now suggested to become minimally proficient. This is, of course, along with quality didactic education.

Q. What is the best way to find a job in this field?

A. Sonographers are in need just about anywhere. Hospitals, medical centers, doctors' offices, and commercial manufacturers are looking for sonographers at this time. Commercial employment usually requires experience prior to entrance into this area of employment.

Applicants need to be certified by the American Registry of Diagnostic Medical Sonographers to be considered by most employers.

Q. What would you say are the most important skills and personal qualities for someone in your field?

A. The roles and qualities needed in a sonographer are best described by Marveen Craig in her book *Introduction to Ultrasonography and Patient Care* (W.B. Saunders, 1993). To summarize these qualities: intellectual curiosity, eagerness and perseverance, quick-thinking and analytic capabilities, good technical orientation, good physical health, self-direction, emotional stability, good communication skills, and dedication.

Q. What advice would you give to someone who is interested in pursuing this type of career?

A. Be sure to check to see if the program you wish to enter is CAAHEP accredited. Lists of these programs can be found at http://www.caahep.org. There are many nonaccredited programs that are very expensive, and the graduate may not even be able to sit for American Registry of Diagnostic Medical Sonographers certification examinations. Checking for prerequisites for certification examinations is important and can be found at http://www.ardms.org.

Dialysis Technicians

OVERVIEW

Dialysis technicians, also called *nephrology technicians* or *renal dialysis technicians*, set up and operate hemodialysis artificial kidney machines for patients with chronic renal failure (CRF). CRF is a condition where the kidneys cease to function normally. Many people, especially diabetics or people who suffer from undetected high blood pressure, develop this condition. These patients require hemodialysis to sustain life. In hemodialysis the patient's blood is circulated through the dialysis machine, which filters out impurities, wastes, and excess fluids from the blood. The cleaned blood is then returned to the body. Dialysis technicians also maintain and repair this equipment as well as help educate the patient and family about dialysis.

HISTORY

Chemist Thomas Graham discovered the process of dialysis in 1854. In his early experiments, Graham separated crystalloids from colloids. Crystalloids are chemical salts that dissolve in a solution, and colloids are jellylike materials that remain uniformly suspended in a solution and will not dissolve. Graham passed crystalloids in a solution through a membrane into another solution. He then recovered the crystalloids by evaporating the solution. Graham predicted possible medical uses for his discovery, but did not do any experiments involving animals or humans.

In 1913, John J. Abel and Leonard G. Rowntree utilized Graham's principle of dialysis in laboratory experiments using animals. They were able to successfully remove chemicals from the animals' blood.

Researchers called the process hemodialysis. *Hemo* comes from the Greek word *haima*, which means blood.

In the early 1940s, scientists developed artificial kidney machines that performed hemodialysis on patients. Improvements in equipment and the development of heparin, a drug that prevents clotting, made hemodialysis practical for the treatment of people with CRF. Before the invention of the artificial kidney machine, patients with CRF would die of uremic poisoning as toxic products built up in their bloodstream.

Just as Graham predicted, the artificial kidney machine separates crystalloids from colloids in a patient's blood. The machine pumps blood from the body through a dialyzer, and then the blood passes through tubes constructed of artificial membranes. The surfaces of the membranes are bathed with a solution called the dialysate. Normal body waste chemicals act as crystalloids and pass through the membranes. However, the blood cells and other proteins act as colloids, which means that they do not pass through the membranes. The blood cells and proteins return to the body with the blood, but without the harmful waste chemicals. The rate of the waste removal depends on the extent of the individual patient's kidney failure, the concentration of waste products in the patient's blood, and the nature and strength of the dialysate.

By the late 1950s hemodialysis was available in health care facilities throughout the United States. During the 1960s, further advances made it possible for dialysis to be successfully carried out in the homes of patients.

While home dialysis is more economical than hospital dialysis, it is still an extremely expensive process. For that reason, Medicare funds have paid for dialysis carried out in health facilities since 1973 and now pay for the equipment patients need for home dialysis.

Whether in the hospital or at home, a patient receiving hemodialysis must be closely monitored by a dialysis technician.

THE JOB

The National Association of Nephrology Technicians/Technologists (NANT) recognizes three types of dialysis technicians: the *patient-care technician,* the *biomedical equipment technician,* and the *dialyzer reprocessing (reuse) technician.*

Dialysis patient-care technicians are responsible for preparing the patient for dialysis, monitoring the procedure, and responding to any emergencies that occur during the treatment. Before dialysis, the technician measures the patient's vital signs (including weight, pulse, blood pressure, and temperature) and obtains blood samples and specimens as required. The technician then inserts tubes into access routes, such as a vein or a catheter, which will exchange blood between the patient and the artificial kidney machine throughout the dialysis session.

While monitoring the process of dialysis, the technician must be attentive, precise, and alert. He or she measures and adjusts blood-flow rates as well as checks and rechecks the patient's vital signs. All of this information is carefully recorded in a log. In addition, the technician must respond to any alarms that occur during the procedure and make appropriate adjustments to the dialysis machine. Should an emergency occur during the session, the technician must be able to administer cardiopulmonary resuscitation (CPR) or other life-saving techniques.

Biomedical equipment technicians are responsible for maintaining and repairing the dialysis machines. Dialyzer reuse technicians care for the dialyzers—the apparatus through which the blood is filtered. Each one must be cleaned and bleached after use, then sterilized by filling it with formaldehyde overnight so that it is ready to be used again for the patient's next treatment. To prevent contamination, a dialyzer may only be reused with the same patient, so accurate records must be kept. Some dialysis units reuse plastic tubing as well; this, too, must be carefully sterilized.

While most hemodialysis takes place in a hospital or special dialysis centers, the use of dialysis in the patient's home is becoming more common. In these cases, technicians travel to patients' homes to carry out the dialysis procedures or to instruct family members in assisting with the process.

In many dialysis facilities the duties described above overlap. The dialysis technician's role is determined by a number of factors: the dialysis facility's management plan, the facility's leadership and staff, the technician's skills and background, the unit's equipment and facilities, and the long-term care plans for patients. However, all dialysis technicians work under the supervision of physicians or registered nurses.

REQUIREMENTS
High School
If you are interested in working as a dialysis technician, you should take biology, chemistry, and health classes while in high school. Mathematics classes will also be beneficial, since you will be working with numbers and equations as you determine the appropriate treatment for each patient. English classes will help you develop your communication skills and improve your ability to follow directions and record information. You may also want to take computer classes so that you are comfortable working with this equipment. Finally, consider taking any class, such as psychology, that will give you insight into dealing with people.

Postsecondary Training

Although there is a movement toward providing more formal academic training in the field of renal dialysis, presently only a few two-year dialysis preparatory programs exist in technical schools and junior colleges. Many people entering the field have some type of experience in a patient-care setting or college training in biology, chemistry, or health-related fields. By far, the majority of technicians learn their skills through on-the-job training at the first hospital or dialysis center where they are employed. Therefore, you should be extremely inquisitive, willing to learn, and able to work as a team member. Inquire at local hospitals and dialysis centers to find out what type of training they offer and their admission requirements. Training may range from several weeks to a year or more. Typically, the training programs include class study on such topics as anatomy, principles of dialysis, and patient care, as well as supervised clinical practice.

Certification or Licensing

In most states, dialysis technicians are not required to be registered, certified, or licensed. However, several states, such as California and New Mexico, do require practicing dialysis technicians to have certification; in addition, a growing number of states are considering legislation to make certification mandatory. In some states, technicians are required to pass a test before they can work with patients. You will need to check with your state's department of health or licensing board to determine specific requirements for your area.

The Board of Nephrology Examiners, Nursing and Technology (BONENT) and the National Nephrology Certification Organization (NNCO) offer a voluntary program of certification for nurses and technicians. The program's purposes are to identify safe, competent practitioners, to promote excellence in the quality of care available to kidney patients, and encourage study and advance the science of nursing and technological fields in nephrology. These organizations hope that eventually all dialysis technicians will be certified.

Technicians who wish to become certified must be high school graduates. You must either have a minimum of one year of experience and be currently working in a dialysis facility or have successfully completed an accredited dialysis course. The certification examination contains questions related to anatomy and physiology, principles of dialysis, treatment and technology related to the care of patients with end-stage renal disease, and general medical knowledge. Certified technicians use the letters CHT (certified hemodialysis technician) after their names. Recertification is required every four years.

To be recertified, dialysis technicians must continue working in the field and present evidence of having completed career-related continuing education.

Other Requirements

The ability to talk easily with patients and their families is essential. Kidney patients, especially those who are just beginning dialysis, are confronting a major—and permanent—life change. You must be able to help them deal with the emotional as well as the physical effects of their condition. Good interpersonal skills are crucial, not only in the technician-patient relationship, but in working closely with other technicians and health care professionals as well. Because the slightest mistake can have deadly consequences, a technician must be thorough and detail oriented. Since the technician is responsible for the lives of patients, you must be mature, able to respond to stressful situations calmly, and think quickly in an emergency. A good head for mathematics and familiarity with the metric system are required. You must be able to calibrate machines and calculate the correct amounts and proportions of solutions to be used as well as quickly determine any necessary changes if there are indications that a patient is not responding to the treatment appropriately.

It can be upsetting to work with people who are ill, and if you have a cheerful disposition and pleasant manner this will help ease the patient's anxiety.

EXPLORING

Volunteering in a hospital, nursing home, dialysis center, or other patient-care facility can give you a taste of what it is like to care for patients. You will soon discover whether you have the necessary disposition to help patients heal both physically and emotionally. Most hospitals have volunteer programs that are open to high school students.

Students interested in the requirements for becoming a dialysis technician may obtain job descriptions from NANT and BONENT. If your interest lies specifically in the area of nursing, you may want to contact the American Nephrology Nurses' Association (ANNA). Also, several journals discuss the professional concerns of those working in the field as well as other issues such as treatments and quality control.

Until there are a greater number of organized and accredited training programs, those who are interested in the career of the dialysis technician must seek information about educational opportunities from local sources such as high school guidance centers, public libraries, and occupational counselors at technical and community colleges. Specific information is best obtained from dialysis centers, dialysis units of local hospitals, home health care agencies, medical societies, schools of nursing, or individual nephrologists.

EMPLOYERS

Dialysis technicians work throughout the country. They are employed by hospitals, nursing homes, dialysis centers, and health care agencies.

STARTING OUT

The best way to enter this field is through a formal training program in a hospital or other training facility. You may also contact your local hospital and dialysis center to determine the possibility of on-the-job training. Some hospitals pay trainees as they learn.

Other ways to enter this field are through schools of nurse assisting, practical nursing, or nursing programs for emergency medical technicians. The length of time required to progress through the dialysis training program and advance to higher levels of responsibility should be shorter if you first complete a related training program. Most dialysis centers offer a regular program of in-service training for their employees.

ADVANCEMENT

Dialysis technicians who have gained knowledge, skills, and experience advance to positions of greater responsibility within their units and can work more independently. They may also work in supervisory positions. The NANT guidelines encourage a distinction between technicians and technologists, with the latter having additional training and broader responsibilities. Some technologists conduct biochemical analyses or research studies to improve equipment. Not all dialysis units make this distinction.

A technician looking for career advancement in the patient-care sector may elect to enter nurses' training; many states require that supervisory personnel in this field are registered nurses. Social, psychological, and counseling services appeal to others who find their greatest satisfaction in interacting with patients and their families.

A dialysis technician interested in biomedical equipment may advance by focusing on machine technology and return to college for a degree in engineering or another related field.

EARNINGS

Earnings for dialysis technicians are dependent on such factors as their job performance, responsibilities, locality, and length of service. Some employers pay higher wages to certified technicians than to those who are not certified. Dialysis technicians earn between $10 and $18 an hour, or $20,800–$37,400 a year for full-time work. According to the U.S. Bureau of Labor Statistics, the average salary in 2000 for employees in private dialysis centers was $33,398. Employees of local government dialysis centers earned an average of $28,580. Technicians who rise to management positions can earn from $35,000 to $40,000.

Technicians receive the customary benefits of vacation, sick leave or personal time, and health insurance. Many hospitals or health care centers not only offer in-service training but also pay tuition and other education costs as an incentive to further self-development and career advancement.

WORK ENVIRONMENT

Dialysis technicians most often work in a hospital or special dialysis centers. The work environment is usually a clean and comfortable patient-care setting. Some technicians are qualified to administer dialysis in patients' homes, and their jobs may require some local travel. Patients who use dialysis at home need education, assistance, and monitoring. Also, technicians may have to take care of patients when trained family members cannot.

A dialysis technician works a 40-hour week. Patients who work full time or part time often arrange to take their dialysis treatments at times that least interfere with their normal activities, therefore some evening and weekend shifts may be required. Flex-time is common in some units, offering four- and even three-day workweeks. Technicians in hospitals may be on call nights or weekends to serve in emergencies.

The spread of hepatitis and the growing risk of HIV infection have necessitated extra precautions in the field of hemodialysis, as in all fields whose procedures involve possible contact with human blood. All technicians must observe universal precautions, which include the wearing of a protective apron, foot covers, gloves, and a full face shield.

The work of a technician can also be physically strenuous, especially if the patient is very ill. However, the equipment is mobile and easily moved.

Because the field of renal dialysis is constantly evolving, technicians must keep themselves up to date with technological advances and incorporate new technology as it becomes available. One advantage of being a certified technician is that organizations such as NANT, BONENT, and ANNA provide journals and offer educational seminars to members.

Although the daily tasks of a dialysis technician can be monotonous, the patients and staff are a diverse group of people. Patients come from all walks of life, all ages, and all levels of society. There is also a great satisfaction in helping critically ill patients stay alive and active. Some patients are carried through a temporary crisis by dialysis treatments and return to normal after a period of time. Other patients may be best treated by kidney transplants. But while they wait for a suitable donated kidney, their lives depend on dialysis treatment.

OUTLOOK

There should continue to be a need for dialysis technicians in the future as the number of people with kidney disease and failure increases. The principal cause of kidney failure, according to the National Kidney Foundation, is diabetes. In 2001, approximately 16 million Americans had diabetes, and the National Kidney Foundation projects this number to increase to 22 million by 2025. Those with kidney failure must have either dialysis or a kidney transplant in order to live. This steadily increasing number of patients in need will mean a continued demand for dialysis technicians.

Technicians make up the largest proportion of the dialysis team, since they can care for only a limited number of patients at a time (the ratio of patient-care technicians to nurses is generally about four to one). There is also a high turnover rate in the field of dialysis technicians, creating many new job openings. Lastly, there is a shortage of trained dialysis technicians in most localities.

A factor that may decrease employment demand is the further development of procedures that may remove the need for dialysis treatments in health care facilities. For instance, if the number of individuals able to participate in home dialysis increases, the staffing requirements and number of dialysis facilities would be affected. Similarly, the growing use of peritoneal dialysis threatens the need for dialysis technicians. In this process the membrane used is the peritoneum (the lining of the abdomen), and the dialysis process takes place within, rather than outside, the patient's body. An increase in the number of kidney transplants could also slow the future demand for dialysis technicians. However, the number of people waiting for transplants is far greater than the number of organs available. Until researchers discover a cure for kidney disease, dialysis technicians will be needed to administer treatment.

FOR MORE INFORMATION

For information on job opportunities, awards, legislative news, and nephrology nursing, contact or visit the following website:
American Nephrology Nurses' Association
East Holly Avenue, Box 56
Pitman, NJ 08071-0056
Tel: 856-256-2320
Email: anna@ajj.com
http://anna.inurse.com

For more information about certification, contact
Board of Nephrology Examiners, Nursing and Technology
PO Box 15945-282
Lenexa, KS 66285
Tel: 913-541-9077
http://www.goamp.com/bonent

Contact this association for information on scholarships, certification, and the career.
National Association of Nephrology Technicians/Technologists
PO Box 2307
Dayton, OH 45401-2307
Tel: 877-607-6268
Email: nant@nant.meinet.com
http://www.dialysistech.org

The NKF is a voluntary health organization involved with educating the public about kidney and urinary tract diseases as well as organ transplantation. For news relating to these issues, fact sheets, and The Electronic Kidney, *an online newsletter, check out the following website:*
National Kidney Foundation (NKF)
30 East 33rd Street, Suite 1100
New York, NY 10016
Tel: 800-622-9010
Email: info@kidney.org
http://www.kidney.org

Dietetic Technicians

QUICK FACTS

School Subjects
Biology
Chemistry

Personal Skills
Helping/teaching
Technical/scientific

Work Environment
Primarily indoors
Primarily one location

Minimum Education Level
Associate's degree

Salary Range
$13,200 to $21,340 to
$34,170+

Certification or Licensing
Recommended

Outlook
Faster than the average

DOT
077

GOE
05.05.17

NOC
3132

O*NET-SOC
29-2051.00

OVERVIEW

Dietetic technicians work in hospitals, nursing homes, public health nutritional programs, food companies, and other institutional settings that require food-service management and nutritional-care services. They usually work under the direction of a dietitian or nutritionist, as members of a team. The two basic types of work for technicians are food-service administration and clinical nutrition. There are approximately 28,000 dietetic technicians employed in the United States.

HISTORY

Dietetics is the study of food preparation, diet planning, and the impact of nutrition on health and well-being. What was perhaps the first scientific nutritional discovery leading to our modern understanding in this field occurred in 1780. Antoine Lavoisier, sometimes called the father of nutrition, and Pierre-Simon LaPlace realized that metabolism, the physiological process in which food is broken down and used, is a form of combustion. This discovery, coupled with Lavoisier's other work in the field, opened the way to much fruitful research into how and why fats, carbohydrates, and proteins affect health.

By the late 19th century, there was a great deal of knowledge concerning the benefits of good nutrition and proper food handling. People also became aware of the importance of various minerals in the diet. The public's interest in nutrition became substantial. Around the turn of the century, several hospitals began to teach dietetics to nurses, stressing cookery as a means of therapy for the sick. Other workers were hired as specialists to prepare food for hospital patients in accordance with the most advanced knowledge of the day. The modern field of dietetics grew out of such early hospital work.

In 1917, the American Dietetic Association (ADA) was formed with 39 charter members. It worked to promote and disseminate educational materials to the public in order to improve the dietary habits of individuals and groups. Today, it still serves as the principal professional organization for advancing the fields of dietetics and nutrition.

As the field of dietetics grew, it encompassed a wider range of activities; several separate categories of workers evolved, differentiated by their level of training and their type of activity. Two important levels of workers now are dietitians and dietetic technicians. The position of dietetic technician is a relatively recent innovation, dating back to the early 1970s. It was designed to provide assistance to dietitians and relieve them of some of their more routine tasks, allowing them to concentrate on work that only they are trained to do. The separate status of dietetic technicians was given a boost in 1972 by a report by the Study Commission on Dietetics, an affiliate of the ADA, that urged various changes in the field and greater coordination of dietetics with other allied health professions.

THE JOB

Dietetic technicians work in a variety of settings, including hospitals, nursing homes, public health agencies, weight-management clinics, correctional facilities, and food companies. They serve in two basic areas: as service personnel in food-service administration and as assistants in clinical nutrition, which is the nutritional care of individuals. Some dietetic technicians are involved in both kinds of activities, while others concentrate on just one area. Specific duties and responsibilities vary widely, depending on where technicians work and the area in which they specialize.

In food-service administration, dietetic technicians often supervise other food-service employees and oversee the food-production operation on a day-to-day basis. They may act as administrative assistants to dietitians, helping implement cost-control measures, developing job specifications and job descriptions, and monitoring the quality of the food and service provided. They may also be responsible for planning menus.

In a medical center, where the food-service staff prepares thousands of meals daily for patients and personnel, there may be a team of dietetic technicians, as well as dietetic aides, assistants, and other food-service workers, all working under the direction of dietitians. In such cases, each dietetic technician may specialize in just one or two activities. On the other hand, in a small organization such as some nursing, Head Start, or geriatric care programs, there may be just one dietetic technician responsible for the overall management of the food-service staff and also for some nutrition counseling. The technician in a small facility may be supervised only by a consultant dietitian and may report directly to the administrator or director of the institution.

Dietetic technicians working in food-service administration plan and prepare schedules and activities, perhaps spending a substantial part of their time on the phone or doing paperwork. They delegate work and plan schedules for other employees, and they train new staff members in food-production methods and the use of kitchen equipment. Later, they follow up by helping prepare evaluations of the food program and assessments of the efficiency of employees or particular production processes.

They also help to develop recipes, adapting standard versions to the particular needs and circumstances of their institution. They write modified diet plans for patients, and they sometimes help patients select their menus. They keep track of food items on hand, process routine orders to the suppliers, order miscellaneous supplies as needed, and supervise food storage. They are involved with departmental budget-control measures and may participate in dietary department conferences.

At other times, dietetic technicians work more directly in the kitchen, overseeing and coordinating actual food-production activities, including the preparation of special therapeutic food items. They may even participate in the preparation of meals, although they usually just monitor the preparations. They supervise dietetic aides, who distribute food in the cafeteria and serve meals to patients in their rooms. Depending on their employers, some dietetic technicians are also responsible for meeting standards in sanitation, housekeeping, safety in equipment operation, and security procedures.

Dietetic technicians who specialize in nutrition care and counseling work under the direction of a clinical or community dietitian. They often work in a health care facility, where they observe and interview patients about their eating habits and food preferences. Dietetic technicians then report diet histories to the dietitians, along with the patients' progress reports. The information is used to outline any changes needed in basic diet plans and menus. They also supervise the serving of food to ensure that meals are nutritionally adequate and conform to the physicians' prescriptions.

Technicians teach the basic principles of sound nutrition, food selection and preparation, and good eating habits to patients and their families so that after leaving the health care facility the patients may continue to benefit. Later, the technicians contact those patients to see how well they are staying on the modified diets and to help them make any further adjustments in accordance with their preferences, habits at home, and the physicians' prescriptions.

Those specializing in nutrition care work in community programs rather than inside a hospital or other inpatient health care facility. If employed by a public health department, clinic, youth center, visiting nurse association, home health agency, or similar organization, dietetic technicians have many of the same counseling duties as they would in an inpatient institutional setting. They may work with low-income families, teaching the economics of food purchasing, preparation, and nutrition. Or they may help the elderly, parents of small children, or other special groups who develop characteristic dietary questions and problems.

Dietetic technicians make follow-up home visits to check on their clients' menu plans, food buying, and cooking skills. In some cases, they help establish permanent arrangements for continuing nutrition care for the needy, such as hot meals for the housebound or school lunch programs.

Another aspect of the job for those working in a community program is the development and coordination of a community education effort. To do this, technicians help prepare brochures and teaching materials or plan classes in nutrition-related topics. In some cases, they even teach classes. Technicians also contact and work with other community groups to promote interest in nutrition.

Some dietetic technicians work in other settings, such as schools, colleges, industrial food-service establishments, and other organizations where large quantities of food are regularly prepared. These positions require technicians to use many of the same administrative skills but do not emphasize meeting special dietary needs of individuals or the educational and counseling aspect of nutritional-care work. Other dietetic technicians are employed in research kitchens, working under the supervision of a dietitian, to perform support activities. As part of their duties they check inventory and order stocks of ingredients, inspect equipment to be sure it is functioning properly, weigh and package food items, check for inaccuracies in precise procedures, and maintain records.

REQUIREMENTS

High School

The educational preparation required for this career includes a high school diploma or its equivalent, plus completion of a two-year,

Commission on Accreditation for Dietetics Education (CADE)-approved program leading to an associate's degree.

During high school, you should emphasize science courses in your studies. Biology and chemistry should provide a good background for both success in college classes and on the job. Mathematics, business, and computer science courses will also prepare you for aspects of this work, such as record keeping, purchasing of supplies, and adjusting recipes. The ADA suggests that you take sociology and psychology classes to broaden your understanding of human behavior. English classes will help you improve your communication skills, which will be very important when working as part of a health care team and with a variety of clients.

Postsecondary Training

The associate's degree program, which is available in many junior and community colleges, combines classroom studies with practical instruction and experience in the field under real working conditions. There are approximately 70 dietetic technician training programs that have been approved by CADE.

When attending an associate's degree program, you can expect to take a mix of general education courses, such as English, biological sciences, humanities, social sciences, and business mathematics, as well as technical courses. The technical instruction is likely to include such topics as normal nutrition and menu planning, therapeutic diets, food preparation, nutrition counseling, quantity food production, and food purchasing and storage.

During a two-year college program, you also get a certain amount of supervised clinical experience, sometimes called a practicum. This provides a close look at the work of a dietetic technician and experience that will be valuable during postgraduate employment. For your practicum, you may be assigned to a patient-care facility, where you help with preparing schedules, ordering food, cooking, or instructing patients. If you are assigned to a health agency, you might accompany a nutritionist on home visits, help with teaching individuals, assist in demonstrating cooking techniques to groups, or observe and analyze information on the types of food people purchase at local grocery stores.

Certification or Licensing

Although dietetic technicians are not required to be licensed or certified, those who have completed an approved education program are eligible to take a certifying examination. Many choose to do so, since holding the DTR designation (dietetic technician, registered) indicates a certain level of competence and can be beneficial in finding a job. The exam is given by the Commission on Dietetic Registration, an agency of the ADA. Registered technicians are required to earn 50 hours of continuing education credit every five years in order to maintain their credentials.

Other Requirements

Anyone considering this line of work should have an interest in nutrition and a desire to serve people. Communication skills also are vital since the job often involves working closely with patients and coworkers. You should be patient and understanding, since you may have to deal with people who are ill or uncooperative. You need to have a knack for planning and organizing and must also be able to follow orders and instructions carefully. Finally, technicians must be adaptable and ready to explore new ideas and methods, because food products, equipment, and administrative practices are constantly changing.

EXPLORING

High school students interested in dietetics should try to find a part-time, summer, or even volunteer job in the food-service department of a hospital or other health care organization. This kind of position enables you to observe the work of the dietary department and to ask questions of people involved in the field. A job in a nonhospital food service, even a restaurant kitchen, could also be of value. With the help of teachers or counselors, you may arrange to meet with a dietitian or dietetic technician for an informational interview.

EMPLOYERS

Dietetic technicians work in hospitals, nursing homes, public health nutritional programs, food companies, clinics, youth centers, visiting nurse associations, home health agencies, and other institutional settings that require food-service management and nutritional-care services. Most technicians work in health care facilities such as hospitals and nursing homes, although some are employed in health agencies such as public health departments, neighborhood health centers, or home health agencies. Schools, correctional facilities, food vendors, and health clubs are also examples of institutions that may have a dietetic staff.

Other employers of dietetic technicians include schools, colleges, industrial food-service establishments, and other organizations where large quantities of food are regularly prepared.

STARTING OUT

Contacts gained during the clinical experience segment of a training program are often good sources of first jobs for dietetic technicians. Applying to the personnel offices of potential employers can be another productive approach. Other good places to check are school placement offices, job listings in health care journals, newspaper classified ads, and private and public employment agencies.

In some areas close to schools that offer dietetic technician training programs, the local labor market is oversupplied. In these cases, graduates may have better results if they extend their job search to areas where competition is less intense.

ADVANCEMENT

Beginning dietetic technicians are usually closely supervised because there is so much to learn about the operations of their new employers. After a time, however, the technicians are often able to take on greater responsibilities and earn higher pay. Often, technicians who have proven their abilities are allowed to perform some of the same functions as entry-level dietitians, such as prescribing diets or diagnosing nutritional problems. With the expanded range of duties, a technician may earn higher pay, while either keeping the same title or officially changing positions. For example, a dietetic technician could be promoted to the position of kitchen manager.

Some dietetic technicians return to school on a full- or part-time basis to complete a bachelor's degree program in a related field such as dietetics, nutrition, food science, or food-service management. To become a dietitian, a year of internship is necessary in addition to the bachelor's degree.

EARNINGS

Earnings vary widely depending on the employer, the education, the experience of the dietetic technician, and the nature of his or her responsibilities. Generally, however, salaries in this field have been increasing for the past few years, and this trend is expected to continue.

According to the U.S. Department of Labor, dietetic technicians had median annual earnings of $21,340 in 2000. Salaries ranged from less than $13,200 to more than $34,170.

Salaries may be influenced by the area—clinical or administrative—in which a dietetic technician specializes. Technicians working in clinical nutrition, involving client assessment and counseling, generally earn less than those working in food and nutrition administration, involving the supervision of food service employees and overseeing food production.

Fringe benefits will depend on the employer, but they usually include paid vacations and holidays, health insurance plans, and meals during working hours.

WORK ENVIRONMENT

Dietary departments in health care facilities are generally well lighted, clean, well ventilated, and near the kitchen areas. Kitchens and serving areas, however, may be intensely active at peak hours and are often very hot, steamy, and noisy. Most dietetic technicians in foodservice administration jobs work 40-hour weeks, in eight-hour shifts, and may be required to work some nights, weekends, or on an irregular schedule, depending on the type of employer. Shifts are usually divided into three eight-hour periods, with each shift responsible for preparing one major meal.

Dietetic technicians in food service may be on their feet most of the time. In some cases, there may be intense pressure to work quickly and accurately. At such times, technicians must be able to give full attention to the details of their own job while coordinating the work of other employees. Often, technicians must fill in for or find replacements for workers who don't show up for their shifts.

Dietetic technicians employed in nutrition care are likely to have more regular hours and a smoother work pace. They spend a great deal of time talking with patients and their families. While the majority of patients are pleasant, on occasion the technician may encounter patients who are difficult or frustrating. Those who work for community programs may even be required to make visits to their clients' homes.

For someone who enjoys food and helping people, this field can be very satisfying. Sometimes, however, technicians confront failure in the kitchen; the work may seem endless and routine; and it is necessary to face the fact that good nutrition cannot solve all health problems. Nonetheless, many dietetic technicians find that the sense of achievement outweighs such negatives.

OUTLOOK

Although the demand for dietetic technicians has been uneven for the past several years, the current outlook is good for the near future. The *Occupational Outlook Handbook* reports that dietetic technicians' employment should grow faster than the average through 2010. This growth is due in part to the strong emphasis placed on nutrition and health in this country and the fact that more health services will be used in future years. The population is growing, and the percentage of older people, who need the most health services, is increasing even faster.

Another reason for the positive outlook for dietetic technicians is that health care organizations now realize the advantages of utilizing them for many jobs. Many of the tasks dietitians used to perform can be done well by dietetic technicians, leaving dietitians to do more specialized work. In addition, dietetic technicians are less expensive to hire and are therefore more cost-efficient for the employer. Job opportunities will most likely be best for those technicians who have received their certification.

FOR MORE INFORMATION

For information on career development, continuing education, and scholarships, contact
American Dietetic Association
216 West Jackson Boulevard, Suite 800
Chicago, IL 60606-6995
Tel: 312-899-0040
Email: education@eatright.org
http://www.eatright.org

To learn more about nutrition, visit the United States Department of Agriculture website.
Center for Nutrition Policy and Promotion
http://www.usda.gov/cnpp

━━━━━━━━━━━ INTERVIEW ━━━━━━━━━━━

Vicki Erdmann is the coordinator of and instructor in the dietetic technology program at Normandale Community College in Bloomington, Minnesota. She has worked in the dietetics profession for nearly 30 years in such positions as hospital clinical dietitian, research dietitian, and dietitian and materials management officer in the U.S. Army Reserve. Vicki spoke to the editors of Careers in Focus: Medical Technicians *about her career and the dietetics field.*

Q. How did you first become interested in this field?
A. During high school, I began working in a hospital kitchen to earn money for college. I became interested in the field while serving modified diets to patients; I was very fortunate to have a dietitian who served as my mentor and encouraged me to pursue the field as a career. I was given many opportunities on the job to

learn the various aspects of hospital dietetics, including working in the kitchen, ordering food, picking up and correcting menus, and even performing some basic patient education. The more I learned, the more excited I became about the field.

Q. What are a dietetic technician's main job responsibilities?
A. It varies depending on the setting one works in. A clinical dietetic technician will have contact with patients/residents/clients and other health professionals, especially nurses. That individual will interview clients to determine food preferences, assist in conducting nutritional screening and assessment to determine the client's needs for nutritional intervention and education, and then implement and evaluate the effectiveness of the care being provided.

Dietetic technicians can also work in food service management, where they are involved with planning menus and overseeing meal service. This involves ordering food, supervising the production and service of meals, maintaining food quality controls and kitchen cleanliness, budgeting, staffing, and training.

Dietetic technicians can also work in community settings, including WIC, extension service, senior feeding programs, and child care feeding programs. They are also employed in school food service, food manufacturing industry, health clubs, and weight loss clinics.

Q. What have your work environments been like?
A. Working in hospitals is very fast-paced! There are deadlines to meet so that menus and food are ready for meal service at the proper time. You are constantly interacting with other health professionals, including nurses, doctors, physical therapists, occupational therapists, and others. You are seeing many patients each day to check their tolerance to their diet and to provide nutritional intervention and education as needed. You will also spend a great deal of time documenting the care you are providing.

Q. How has your job changed since entering the dietetics field?
A. When I entered the field I wanted to work as part of a health care team in a large teaching hospital. I did so for several years and greatly enjoyed it. I would probably still be doing so today, had I not had the opportunity to teach. Teaching is another area that I greatly enjoy, and that is what I have been doing now for over 25 years. Teaching dietetic technician students still allows me

to participate in patient care in the hospital setting while working with my students, so in a way, it is the best of both worlds.

Q. What kind of education and training did you pursue for your career? What kinds of things do students learn in your program?

A. I pursued an undergraduate major in dietetics and a master's in nutritional science. Upon completion of my B.S. degree, I completed a nine-month dietetic internship. As a dietetics major, you will study foods, nutrition, education, human development, chemistry, anatomy, physiology, oral and written communications, computers, sociology, psychology, management, and medical terminology.

Q. What is the best way to find a job in this field?

A. Networking. Being a member of professional organizations, serving on committees, and volunteering in the community is the best way to make contacts with others in the profession. In dietetics, many jobs are advertised by word of mouth.

Q. What would you say are the most important skills and personal qualities for a dietetic technician?

A. • People skills. The ability to meet and communicate with a variety of people, including health professionals, kitchen staff, patients and clients. One must be comfortable in meeting and working with a variety of people who may have physical and emotional impairments.

• It helps to have some "hands-on" knowledge of cooking and some interest in and awareness of the eating habits of various ethnic groups. You must not be afraid to sample foods of different types.

• Communication skills, both verbal and written, are very important. You must be comfortable talking one to one with coworkers or clients, and also teaching groups of people in a class setting.

• Attention to detail is necessary for documentation, calculations of tube feedings, calorie intakes, etc. You need to be able to include the pertinent information in a succinct and professional manner.

• Ability to work under pressure, meet time deadlines, etc. is critical.

• Skill in a foreign language is extremely useful.

Q. What are the pros and cons of being a dietetic technician?

A. Pros: (1) Working in a field where you gain job satisfaction and professional recognition for your efforts; (2) people are very interested in health and wellness today, and they are eager to learn what you have to share about nutrition; (3) diverse opportunities for employment in a variety of settings, including health care, wellness, and industry; (4) opportunity to use "people skills" and teaching skills.

Cons: (1) Work can be fast-paced and you need to be able to work quickly but still with accuracy. This may create stress for some people. (2) The field of dietetics is relatively low paying for the amount of training required and the level of responsibility involved. But you are not performing direct patient care, such as in nursing (which for some people is a plus); this does account for the low salaries. On the plus side, however, benefits in health care are often very good. (3) Some health professionals lack awareness of the role of the dietetic technician as a nutrition paraprofessional.

Q. What advice would you give to someone who is interested in pursuing this career?

A. Get a job in a health care setting. A hospital or nursing home kitchen is an excellent opportunity to learn. It's hard work and not very glamorous, but it really gives you a feel for the field. As a dietitian, or dietetic technician, you will not necessarily be working in the kitchen, but it is crucial to understand how that end of the operation works so that you can work in collaboration with the kitchen staff in a hospital or nursing home.

Electroneurodiagnostic Technologists

QUICK FACTS

School Subjects
Biology
Mathematics
Physics

Personal Skills
Mechanical/manipulative
Technical/scientific

Work Environment
Primarily indoors
Primarily one location

Minimum Education Level
Some postsecondary training

Salary Range
$25,000 to $37,853 to
$70,000

Certification or Licensing
Recommended

Outlook
Little change or more slowly
than the average

DOT
003

GOE
05.01.01

NOC
3218

O*NET-SOC
N/A

OVERVIEW

Electroneurodiagnostic technologists, sometimes called EEG technologists or END technologists, operate electronic instruments called electroencephalographs. These instruments measure and record the brain's electrical activity. The information gathered is used by physicians (usually neurologists) to diagnose and determine the effects of certain diseases and injuries, including brain tumors, cerebral vascular strokes, Alzheimer's disease, epilepsy, some metabolic disorders, and brain injuries caused by accidents or infectious diseases.

HISTORY

The brain constantly discharges small electrical impulses. These vibrations can be picked up from the surface of the head, amplified, and then recorded on paper. These currents were first detected in England in 1875 by Richard Caton, who used electrodes on the exposed brains of rabbits and monkeys. The resulting picture of electrical brain activity, usually called a tracing, became known as an electroencephalogram.

Other researchers independently studied this brain activity in the late 1800s and early 1900s. In 1929, the German Hans Berger developed the first electroencephalograph to be used on human beings.

In the mid-1930s, electroencephalograms were developed to diagnose epilepsy. Shortly afterward, they were used to locate brain tumors. By the end of the 1930s, a new field had opened up through

66

which doctors and technicians could better diagnose and treat neurological disorders.

THE JOB

The basic principle behind electroencephalography (EEG) is that electrical impulses emitted by the brain, often called brain waves, vary according to the brain's age, activity, and condition. Research has established that certain brain conditions correspond to certain brain waves. Therefore, testing brain waves can aid the neurologist (a physician specially trained in the study of the brain) in making a diagnosis of a person's illness or injury.

The EEG technologist's first task with a new patient is to take a simplified medical history. This entails asking questions and recording answers about his or her past health status and present illness. These answers provide the technologist with necessary information about the patient's condition. They also provide an opportunity to help the patient relax before the test.

The technologist then applies electrodes to the patient's head. Often, technologists must choose the best combination of instrument controls and placement of electrodes to produce the kind of tracing that has been requested. In some cases, a physician will give special instructions to the technologist regarding the placement of electrodes.

Once in place, the electrodes are connected to the recording equipment. Here, a bank of sensitive electronic amplifiers transmits information to writing instruments. Tracings from each electrode are made on a moving strip of paper or recorded on optical disks in response to the amplified impulses coming from the brain. The resulting graph is a recording of the patient's brain waves.

EEG technologists are not responsible for interpreting the tracings—that is the job of the neurologist. However, EEG technologists must be able to recognize abnormal brain activity and any readings on the tracing that are coming from somewhere other than the brain, such as readings of eye movement or nearby electrical equipment.

Technologists can make recording changes to better present the abnormal findings for physician interpretation. Stray readings are known as artifacts. Technologists must be able to determine what kinds of artifacts should be expected for an individual patient on the basis of the patient's medical history or present illness. Technologists should also be sensitive to these artifacts and be able to identify them if they occur.

Technologists must be able to detect faulty recordings made by human error or by machine malfunctions. When mechanical problems occur, technologists should notify their supervisors so that trained equipment technicians can be called to repair the machine.

Throughout the procedure, electroneurodiagnostic technologists observe the patient's behavior and make detailed notes about any aspect of the behavior that might be of use to the physician in interpreting the tracing. They also keep watch on the patient's brain, heart, and breathing functions for any signs that the patient is in any immediate danger.

During the testing, the patient may be either asleep or awake. In some cases, the physician may want recordings taken in both states. Sometimes the physician prescribes drugs or special procedures to simulate a specific kind of condition. Administering the drugs or procedures is often the technologist's responsibility.

EEG technologists need a basic understanding of any medical emergencies that can occur during this procedure. By being prepared, they can react properly if one of these emergencies should arise. For instance, if a patient suffers an epileptic seizure, technologists must know what to do. They must be flexible and able to handle medical crises during procedures.

EEGs are increasingly used on a routine basis in the operating room to monitor patients during major surgery. EEG technologists may also handle other specialized electroencephalograms. For example, in a procedure called ambulatory monitoring, heart and brain activities are tracked over a 24-hour period by a small recording device on the patient's side. In evoked potential testing, a special machine is used to measure the brain's electrical activity in response to specific types of stimuli. In nerve conduction studies, technologists stimulate peripheral nerves with an electrical current and record how long it takes the nerve impulse to reach the muscle. The polysomnogram is a procedure that uses EEG and other physiologic monitors to evaluate sleep and sleep disorders.

Besides conducting various kinds of electroencephalograms, EEG technologists also maintain the EEG machine, perform minor repairs (major repairs require trained equipment technicians), schedule appointments, and order supplies. In some cases, technologists may have some supervisory responsibilities; however, registered electroencephalographic technologists take on most supervisory responsibilities.

REQUIREMENTS

High School

You must have a high school diploma for entry into any kind of EEG technologist training program, whether in school or on the job. In general, you will find it helpful to have three years of mathematics (including algebra) and three years of science (including biology, chemistry, and physics). In addition, you should take courses in English, especially those that help improve communication skills, and in social sciences so that you can better understand the social and psychological needs of your patients.

Postsecondary Training

There are two main types of postsecondary training available for EEG technologists: on-the-job training and formal classroom training. Many technologists who are currently working received on-the-job training; however, EEG equipment is becoming so sophisticated that many employers prefer to hire EEG technologists with prior formal training.

On-the-job training generally lasts from a few months to one year, depending on the employer's special requirements. Trainees learn how to handle the equipment and carry out procedures by observing and receiving instruction from senior electroencephalographic technologists.

Formal training consists of both practice in the clinical laboratory and instruction in the classroom. The classroom instruction usually focuses on basic subjects such as human anatomy, physiology, neuroanatomy, clinical neurology, neuropsychiatry, clinical and internal medicine, psychology, electronics, and instrumentation. The curriculum also includes EEG, evoked potentials, and at least an introduction to nerve conduction and polysomnography. The postsecondary programs usually last from one to two years, offering either a certificate or associate's degree upon completion. Hospitals, medical centers, and community or technical colleges offer these courses. Currently there are 12 schools with accredited two-year programs. According to the American Society of Electroneurodiagnostic Technologists, by 2005 anyone entering the END profession will be required to have an associate's degree or higher and have successfully completed an accredited program reviewed by the Joint Review Committee on Education in Electroneurodiagnostic Technology.

Students who have completed one year of on-the-job training or who have graduated from a formal training program may apply for registration.

Certification or Licensing

The American Board of Registration of Electroencephalographic and Evoked Potential Technologists (ABRET) offers certification as a registered electroencephalographic technologist (REEGT).

Although registration is not required for employment, it is an acknowledgment of the technologist's training and does make advancement easier. Registration may also provide a salary increase.

Other Requirements
EEG technologists need good vision and manual dexterity, an aptitude for working with mechanical and electronic equipment, and the ability to get along well with patients, their families, and members of the hospital staff. To be a successful technologist, you must be good with people, quickly recognize what others may be feeling, and personalize treatment to the individual patient's needs. You need to be able to realize that some patients will be very ill, even in the process of dying.

EXPLORING

Prospective EEG technologists will find it difficult to gain any direct experience on a part-time basis in electroencephalography. Your first direct experience with the work will generally come during on-the-job training sessions or in the practical-experience portion of your formal training. You may, however, be able to gain some general exposure to patient-care activities by signing up for volunteer work at a local hospital. In addition, you can arrange to visit a hospital, clinic, or doctor's office where electroencephalograms are administered. In this way, you may be able to watch technologists at work or talk to them about what the work is like.

EMPLOYERS

Electroneurodiagnostic technologists typically find work in hospitals, medical centers, clinics, and government agencies that perform EEGs.

STARTING OUT

Technologists often obtain permanent employment in the hospital where they received their on-the-job or work-study training. You can also find employment through classified ads in newspapers and by contacting the personnel offices of hospitals, medical centers, clinics, and government agencies that employ EEG technologists.

ADVANCEMENT

Opportunities for advancement are good for registered EEG technologists. Those without registration will find opportunities for advancement severely limited.

Usually, registered electroneurodiagnostic technologists are assigned to conduct more difficult or specialized electroencephalograms. They also supervise other electroencephalographic technologists, arrange work schedules, and teach techniques to new trainees. They may also establish procedures, manage a laboratory, keep records, schedule appointments, and order supplies.

EEG technologists may advance to *chief electroencephalographic technologists* and thus take on even more responsibilities in laboratory management and in teaching new personnel and students. Chief electroencephalographic technologists generally work under the direction of an electroencephalographer, neurologist, or neurosurgeon.

EARNINGS

According to the American Society of Electroneurodiagnostic Technologists, salaries range from $25,000 for new graduates of END programs to more than $70,000 for lab managers of independent contractors. The average salary for all END technologists was $37,853 in 2000. Earnings depend on education, experience, level of responsibility, type of employment, and geographical region. Salaries for registered EEG technologists tended to be higher than nonregistered technologists with equivalent experience.

The highest salaries for EEG technologists tend to go to those who work as laboratory supervisors, teachers in training programs, and program directors in schools of electroencephalographic technology.

Technologists working in hospitals receive the same fringe benefits as other hospital workers, usually including health insurance, paid vacations, and sick leave. In some cases, the benefits may also include educational assistance, pension plans, and uniform allowances.

WORK ENVIRONMENT

EEG technologists usually work five-day, 40-hour workweeks, with only occasional overtime required. Some hospitals require them to be on call for emergencies during weekends, evenings, and holidays. Technologists doing sleep studies may work most of their hours at night.

EEG technologists generally work with people who are ill and may be frightened or emotionally disturbed. As a result, work can be unpredictable and challenging.

Most EEG technologists are employed by hospitals, where the work can vary greatly. In emergency situations, the work is often stressful and hectic as they work closely with other staff members. At other times, conditions are calmer. The EEG technologist often works independently with a patient, spending much time in a darkened room during the tests.

OUTLOOK

Employment of electroneurodiagnostic technologists is expected to grow more slowly than the average, primarily because of new procedures and technologies that require fewer workers to do the same amount of work. Also, hospitals' use of cross-trained employees to cover many jobs will further diminish the need for specially trained technologists. The slow growth should be offset somewhat by population growth and an increase in the use of electroencephalographs in surgery, diagnosis, monitoring, and research. There is some promise of employment for END technologists in the area of polysomnography and long-term monitoring for epilepsy and intraoperative monitoring.

FOR MORE INFORMATION

For information and an application to start the EEG or Evoked Potential examination process, contact
American Board of Registration of Electroencephalographic and Evoked Potential Technologists
1904 Croydon Drive
Springfield, IL 62703
Tel: 217-553-3758
Email: abreteo@aol.com
http://www.abret.org

For a career brochure and information about scholarships and educational opportunities, contact
American Society of Electroneurodiagnostic Technologists
428 West 42nd Street, Suite B
Kansas City, MO 64111
Tel: 816-931-1120
Email: info@aset.org
http://www.aset.org

For information on polysomnograms and sleep disorders, contact
Association of Polysomnographic Technology
PO Box 14861
Lenexa, KS 66285-4861
Tel: 913-541-1991
http://www.aptweb.org

For information on accredited training programs, contact
Joint Review Committee on Electroneurodiagnostic Technology
Route 1, Box 63A
Genoa, WI 54632
Tel: 608-689-2058

Emergency Medical Technicians

OVERVIEW

Emergency medical technicians, often called *EMTs,* respond to medical emergencies to provide immediate treatment for ill or injured persons both on the scene and during transport to a medical facility. They function as part of an emergency medical team, and the range of medical services they perform varies according to their level of training and certification. There are approximately 172,000 emergency medical technicians employed in the United States.

HISTORY

American systems for providing emergency medical services and transport to hospitals did not receive much attention until the 1960s. Prior to that time, ambulance drivers and attendants were often volunteers who had undergone some first-aid training. The quality and quantity of their instruction and experience varied widely, as did the medical equipment they had available in their vehicles. By current-day standards, much of the nation's initial ambulance service was deplorable.

A major milestone was the federal Highway Safety Act of 1966, which included, for the first time, uniform standards for emergency medical services. Another important piece of federal legislation was the Emergency Medical Services System Act of 1973, which authorized funds for research and training. In addition, this act also made money available for organizing regional emergency medical systems.

QUICK FACTS

School Subjects
Biology
Health

Personal Skills
Helping/teaching
Technical/scientific

Work Environment
Indoors and outdoors
Primarily multiple locations

Minimum Education Level
Some postsecondary training

Salary Range
$14,660 to $22,460 to $37,760+

Certification or Licensing
Required by all states

Outlook
Much faster than the average

DOT
079

GOE
10.03.02

NOC
3234

O*NET-SOC
29-2041.00

In 1970, the National Registry of Emergency Medical Technicians (NREMT) was formed. Today, NREMT is an independent agency that establishes qualification levels for EMTs, determines the competency of working EMTs through examination, and offers educational and training programs to promote the improved delivery of emergency medical services. NREMT provides uniform national certification for qualified EMTs who wish to be included in the National Registry.

In 1971, the U.S. Department of Transportation published a national standard basic training course to increase the competence of ambulance personnel. By 1977, all the states had adopted the Department of Transportation course, or a close equivalent, as the basis for state certification. Now, more than 600,000 individuals have taken this basic training course.

THE JOB

EMTs provide on-site emergency care. Their goal is to identify rapidly the nature of the emergency, stabilize the patient's condition, and initiate proper medical procedures at the scene and en route to a hospital. Communities often take great pride in their emergency medical services, knowing that they are as well prepared as possible and that they can minimize the tragic consequences of mishandling emergencies.

EMTs are sent in an ambulance to the scene of an emergency by a *dispatcher,* who acts as a communications channel for all aspects of emergency medical services. The dispatcher may also be trained as an EMT. It typically is the dispatcher who receives the call for help, sends out the appropriate medical resource, serves as the continuing link between the emergency vehicle and medical facility throughout the situation, and relays any requests for special assistance at the scene.

EMTs, who often work in two-person teams, must be able to get to an emergency scene in any part of their geographic area quickly and safely. For the protection of the public and themselves, they must obey the traffic laws that apply to emergency vehicles. They must be familiar with the roads and any special conditions affecting the choice of route, such as traffic, weather-related problems, and road construction.

Once at the scene, they may find victims who appear to have had heart attacks, are burned, trapped under fallen objects, lacerated, in labor, poisoned, or emotionally disturbed. Because people who have been involved in an emergency are sometimes very upset, EMTs often have to exercise skill in calming both victims and bystanders. They must do their work efficiently and in a reassuring manner.

EMTs are often the first qualified personnel to arrive on the scene, so they must make the initial evaluation of the nature and extent of the medical problem. The accuracy of this early assessment can be crucial. EMTs must be on the lookout for any clues, such as medical identification emblems, indicating that the person has significant allergies, diabetes, epilepsy, or other conditions that may affect decisions about emergency treatment. EMTs must know what questions to ask bystanders or family members if they need more information about a patient.

Once they have evaluated the situation and the patient's condition, EMTs establish the priorities of required care. They administer emergency treatment under standing orders or in accordance with specific instructions received over the radio from a physician. For example, they may have to open breathing passages, perform cardiac resuscitation, treat shock, or restrain emotionally disturbed patients. The particular procedures and treatments that EMTs may carry out depend partly on the level of certification they have achieved.

People who must be transported to the hospital are put on stretchers or backboards, lifted into the ambulance, and secured for the ride. The choice of hospital is not always up to the EMTs, but when it is, they must base the decision on their knowledge of the equipment and staffing needed by the patients. The receiving hospital's emergency department is informed by radio, either directly or through the

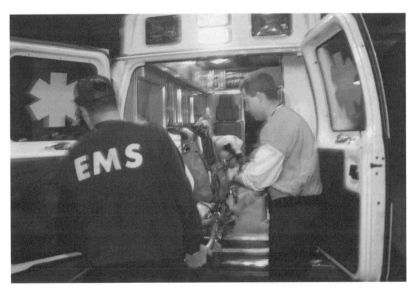

Emergency medical technicians help an accident victim into an ambulance. (*Corbis*)

dispatcher, of details such as the number of persons being transport-ed and the nature of their medical problems. Meanwhile, EMTs con-tinue to monitor the patients and administer care as directed by the medical professional with whom they are maintaining radio contact.

Once at the hospital, EMTs help the staff bring the patients into the emergency department and may assist with the first steps of in-hospital care. They supply whatever information they can, verbally and in writing, for the hospital's records. In the case of a patient's death, they complete the necessary procedures to ensure that the deceased's property is safeguarded.

After the patient has been delivered to the hospital, EMTs check in with their dispatchers and then prepare the vehicle for another emergency call. This includes replacing used linens and blankets; replenishing supplies of drugs, oxygen, and so forth. In addition, EMTs make sure that the ambulance is clean and in good running condition. At least once during the shift, they check the gas, oil, bat-tery, siren, brakes, radio, and other systems.

REQUIREMENTS

High School
While still in high school, interested students should take courses in health and science, driver education, and English. To be admitted to a basic training program, applicants usually must be at least 18 years old and have a high school diploma and valid driver's license. Exact requirements vary slightly between states and training courses. Many EMTs first become interested in the field while in the U.S. Armed Forces, where they may have received training as medics.

Postsecondary Training
The standard basic training program for EMTs was designed by the U.S. Department of Transportation. It is taught in hospitals, com-munity colleges, and police, fire, and health departments across the country. It is approximately 110 hours in length and constitutes the minimum mandatory requirement to become an EMT. In this course, you are taught how to manage common emergencies such as bleed-ing, cardiac arrest, fractures, and airway obstruction. You also learn how to use equipment such as stretchers, backboards, fracture kits, and oxygen delivery systems.

Successful completion of the basic EMT course opens several opportunities for further training. Among these are a two-day course on removing trapped victims and a five-day course on driving emergency vehicles. Another, somewhat longer course, trains dispatchers. Completion of these recognized training courses may be required for EMTs to be eligible for certain jobs in some areas. In addition, EMTs who have graduated from the basic program may work toward meeting further requirements to become registered at one of the two higher levels recognized by the National Registry of Emergency Medical Technicians: EMT-intermediate and EMT-paramedic.

Certification or Licensing
All 50 states have some certification requirement. Certification is only open to those who have completed the standard basic training course. Some states offer new EMTs the choice of the National Registry examination or the state's own certification examination. A majority of states accept national registration in place of their own examination for EMTs who relocate to their states.

At present, the National Registry of Emergency Medical Technicians recognizes three levels of competency: EMT-basic, EMT-intermediate, and EMT-paramedics (or EMT-Ps). Although it is not always essential for EMTs to become registered with one of these three ratings, you can expect better job prospects as you attain higher levels of registration.

Candidates for the basic level of registration, known as EMT-basic, must have completed the standard Department of Transportation training program (or their state's equivalent), have six months' experience, and pass both a state-approved practical examination and a written examination.

The EMT-intermediate level of competency requires all candidates to have current registration at the basic EMT level. You must also have a certain amount of experience and pass both a written test and a practical examination.

To become registered as an EMT-paramedic, the highest level of registration, candidates must be already registered at the basic level. They must have completed a special EMT-P training program, have six months of experience working as an EMT-P, and pass both a written and practical examination. Because training is much more comprehensive and specialized than for other EMTs, EMT-Ps are prepared to make more physician-like observations and judgments. The training program for EMT-Ps is accredited by the Committee on Allied Health Education and Accreditation of the American Medical Association.

EMT-Ps must renew their registration every two years by meeting certain experience and continuing education requirements. Refresher courses are available to help EMT-Ps stay abreast of new techniques and equipment.

Other Requirements

Anyone who is considering becoming an EMT should have a desire to serve people and be emotionally stable and clearheaded. You must inspire confidence with levelheadedness and good judgment. You must be efficient, neither wasting time nor hurrying through delicate work.

Prospective EMTs need to be in good physical condition. Other requirements include good manual dexterity and motor coordination; the ability to lift and carry up to 125 pounds; good visual acuity, with lenses for correction permitted; accurate color vision, enabling safe driving and immediate detection of diagnostic signs; and competence in giving and receiving verbal and written communication.

EXPLORING

Students in high school usually have little opportunity for direct experience with the emergency medical field. It may be possible to learn a great deal about the health-services field through a part-time, summer, or volunteer job in a hospital or clinic. Such service jobs can provide a chance to observe and talk to staff members concerned with emergency medical services.

High school health courses are a useful introduction to some of the concepts and terminology that EMTs use. You may also be able to take a first-aid class or training in cardiopulmonary resuscitation. Organizations such as the Red Cross can provide information on local training courses available.

EMPLOYERS

EMTs are employed by fire departments, private ambulance services, police departments, volunteer emergency medical services squads, hospitals, industrial plants, or other organizations that provide pre-hospital emergency care.

STARTING OUT

A good source of employment leads for a recent graduate of the basic EMT training program is the school or agency that provided the training. You can also apply directly to local ambulance services, fire departments, and employment agencies.

In some areas, you may face stiff competition if you are seeking full-time paid employment immediately upon graduation. Although you may sometimes qualify for positions with fire and police departments, you are generally more likely to be successful in pursuing positions with private companies.

Volunteer work is an option for EMTs. Volunteers are likely to average eight to 12 hours of work per week. If you are a beginning EMT without prior work experience in the health field, you may find it advantageous to start your career as a part-time volunteer to gain experience.

Flexibility about the location of a job may help you gain a foothold on the career ladder. In some areas, salaried positions are hard to find because of a strong tradition of volunteer ambulance services. Therefore, if you are willing to relocate where the demand is higher, you should have a better chance of finding employment.

ADVANCEMENT

With experience, EMTs can gain more responsibility while retaining the same job. However, more significant advancement is possible if you move up through the progression of ratings recognized by the NREMT. These ratings acknowledge increasing qualifications, making higher paying jobs and more responsibility easier to obtain.

An avenue of advancement for some EMTs leads to holding an administrative job, such as supervisor, director, operations manager, or trainer. Another avenue of advancement might be further training in a different area of the health care field. Some EMTs eventually move out of the health care field entirely and into medical sales, where their familiarity with equipment and terminology can make them valuable employees.

EARNINGS

Earnings of EMTs depend on the type of employer and individual level of training and experience. Those working in the public sector, for police and fire departments, usually receive a higher wage than those in the private sector, working for ambulance companies and hospitals. Salary levels typically rise with increasing levels of skill, training, and certification.

According to the U.S. Department of Labor, median annual earnings of EMTs and paramedics were $22,460 in 2000. Salaries ranged from less than $14,660 to more than $37,760. For those who worked in local government the median salary was $24,800; in hospitals, $23,590; and in local and suburban transportation, $20,950.

Benefits vary widely depending on the employer but generally include paid holidays and vacations, health insurance, and pension plans.

WORK ENVIRONMENT

EMTs must work under all kinds of conditions, both indoors and outdoors, and sometimes in very trying circumstances. They must do their work regardless of extreme weather conditions and are often required to do fairly strenuous physical tasks such as lifting, climbing, and kneeling. They consistently deal with situations that many people would find upsetting and traumatic, such as deaths, accidents, and serious injuries.

EMTs usually work irregular hours, including some nights, weekends, and holidays. Those working for fire departments often put in 56 hours a week, while EMTs employed in hospitals, private firms, and police departments typically work a 40-hour week. Volunteer EMTs work much shorter hours.

An additional stress factor faced by EMTs is concern over contracting AIDS or other infectious diseases from bleeding patients. The actual risk of exposure is quite small, and emergency medical programs have implemented procedures to protect EMTs from exposure to the greatest possible degree; however, some risk of exposure does exist, and prospective EMTs should be aware of this.

In spite of the intensity of their demanding job, many EMTs derive enormous satisfaction from knowing that they are able to render such a vital service to the victims of sudden illness or injury.

OUTLOOK

Overall, this industry is expected to grow much faster than the average for all occupations through 2010. However, the employment outlook for paid EMTs depends partly on the community in which they are seeking employment. Many communities perceive the advantages of high-quality emergency medical services and are willing and able to raise tax dollars to support them. In these communities, which are often larger, the employment outlook should remain favorable. Volunteer services are being phased out in these areas, and well-equipped emergency services operated by salaried EMTs are replacing them.

In some communities, however, particularly smaller ones, the employment outlook is not so favorable. Maintaining a high-quality emergency medical services delivery system can be expensive, and financial strains on some local governments could inhibit the growth of these services. Communities may not be able to support the level of emergency medical services that they would otherwise like to, and the employment prospects for EMTs may remain limited.

Another important factor affecting the outlook is that the proportion of older people, who most use emergency medical services, is growing in many communities, placing more demands on the emergency medical services delivery system and increasing the need for EMTs.

FOR MORE INFORMATION

For industry news and government affairs, contact
American Ambulance Association
8201 Greensboro Drive, Suite 300
McLean, VA 22102
Tel: 800-523-4447
http://www.the-aaa.org

For educational programs and scholarship information, contact
National Association of Emergency Medical Technicians
PO Box 1400
Clinton, MS 39060-1400
Tel: 800-346-2368
Email: info@naemt.org
http://www.naemt.org

For information on testing for EMT certification, contact
National Registry of Emergency Medical Technicians
Rocco V. Morando Building
PO Box 29233
6610 Busch Boulevard
Columbus, OH 43229
Tel: 614-888-4484
http://www.nremt.org

Histologic Technicians

QUICK FACTS

School Subjects
Biology
Chemistry
Health

Personal Skills
Following instructions
Technical/scientific

Work Environment
Primarily indoors
Primarily one location

Minimum Education Level
Some postsecondary training

Salary Range
$18,550 to $27,540 to
$42,370+

Certification or Licensing
Required by certain states

Outlook
About as fast as the average

DOT
078

GOE
02.04.02

NOC
3211

O*NET-SOC
29-2012.00

OVERVIEW

Histologic technicians perform basic laboratory procedures to prepare tissue specimens for microscopic examination. They process specimens to prevent deterioration and cut them using special laboratory equipment. They stain specimens with special dyes and mount the tissues on slides. Histologic technicians work closely with *pathologists* and other medical personnel to detect disease and illness.

HISTORY

In 1664, Robert Hooke, an English scientist, used his penknife to slice pieces of cork. He placed these thin sections under the microscope. A few years later, the Dutch naturalist Anton van Leeuwenhoek used his shaving razor to carve thin sections from flowers, a writing quill, and a cow's optic nerve. Both men wanted to observe the microscopic structure of objects. Because of their investigations, the science of histology was born.

THE JOB

Histologic technicians use delicate instruments, which are often computerized, to prepare tissues for microscopic scrutiny and diagnosis. They must also perform quality control tests and keep accurate records of their work.

After a tissue sample is taken, the first step in preparing it for study is known as fixation. A pathologist or scientist usually performs this step. The specimen is examined, described, trimmed to the right size, and placed in special fluids to preserve it.

When the fixed specimen arrives at the histology lab, the histologic technician removes the water and replaces it with melted wax, which moves into the tissue and provides support for the delicate cellular structure as it cools and hardens. Then the technician places small pieces of wax-soaked tissue in larger blocks of wax, a step called embedding, which prevents the tissue from collapsing during the next step of the process.

The technician then sections the specimen by mounting it on a microtome, a scientific instrument with a very sharp blade. The microtome cuts thin slices of tissue, often only one cell thick. The technician cuts many sections of tissue, usually one after another so they form a ribbon, which are then placed in warm water until they flatten out. Then the prepared sections are laid on microscope slides.

Next the technician stains each tissue specimen by adding chemicals and then places a coverslip over the sample to protect it. Different stains highlight different tissue structures or abnormalities in the cells, which aids in the diagnosis and study of diseases.

A second, quicker technique is used to prepare samples and make diagnoses while the patient is still in the operating room. In these

Histology Websites

http://www.histology-world.com
This site offers puzzles, games, quizzes, and slideshows that will help you increase your knowledge of histology. It also includes recommendations for books and other study materials.

http://www.histology.nih.gov
This site offers a public database with annotated images of different kinds of tissue and cells. There is also a discussion board for registered users.

http://www-medlib.med.utah.edu/WebPath/HISTHTML/HISTO.html
This page links to several anatomy and histology tutorials. These tutorials provide insights on the procedures that histologic technicians perform.

http://www.histology.to/
This site is a wealth of information on histology programs, career resources, and online discussion groups, among other things.

cases, tissue specimens are frozen instead of being embedded in wax. It is important for a technician to work swiftly, accurately, and cooperate with the rest of the team during this procedure because surgeries cannot be completed until test results are delivered.

In the laboratory, histologic technicians work with a lot of machines, such as robotic stainers, tissue processors, and cover slippers, but they must have the knowledge to perform all the functions manually should the equipment malfunction. They must also work closely with a team of researchers, as well as other laboratory and medical personnel.

REQUIREMENTS

High School

Biology, chemistry, mathematics, and computer science courses are necessary to develop the preliminary technical skills needed for histotechnology programs. Classes in communication, such as speech and English, are also helpful to reinforce your written and verbal skills.

Postsecondary Training

You can become a histologic technician with a high school diploma and on-the-job training, but a college degree or other formal training is becoming more generally recommended.

You can enter the field with an associate's degree from an accredited college or university and with supervised, hands-on experience in clinical settings. You may also prepare for the profession through a one- or two-year certificate program at an accredited institution, such as a hospital. These programs combine classroom studies along with clinical and laboratory experience.

Certification or Licensing

Certification is not required for entry-level histologic technicians, but it can aid in your hiring and the advancement of your career. The Board of Registry of the American Society of Clinical Pathology is the main certifying organization for professions in laboratory medicine. Applicants can qualify for the Board of Registry exam in three ways. They can complete an accredited program in histotechnology, earn an associate's degree from an accredited college or university and combine it with one year of experience, or have a high school diploma and two years of experience. In January 2005, this last route will no longer be acceptable for qualification; advanced educational training will be required in order to be eligible for certification. Some states also require that all laboratory personnel be licensed; check your individual state department of health for requirements.

Other Requirements

To be a successful histologic technician, you should be patient, attentive to detail, and able to concentrate well under pressure when necessary. Good color vision and manual dexterity are important for the meticulous work involved. Some laboratory work can also be repetitive, requiring technicians to perform the same part of a procedure all day long. Finally, you must be honest and willing to admit mistakes made, because people's lives may depend on how well you do your job.

EXPLORING

A good way to explore the work of histologic technicians is to prepare your own specimens and slides. You can purchase an inexpensive microscope at most toy or hobby shops, and many kits with prepared slides and materials to prepare slides of your own. Taking biology and earth science classes that involve laboratory work will also provide you with the chance to prepare specimens for observation. You can also ask your guidance counselor or science teacher to help you contact a histologic technician to find out about the day-to-day responsibilities of his or her job.

EMPLOYERS

A histologic technician has the opportunity to work in many fields of medicine and science. Most are employed by hospitals or by industrial laboratories that specialize in chemical, petrochemical, pharmaceutical, cosmetic, or household products. Other employers include medical clinics, universities, government organizations, and biomedical companies. Regional laboratories for large health systems hire employees to work flexible shifts since their laboratories operate seven days a week, 24 hours a day. This arrangement could allow a student to attend college classes while working.

STARTING OUT

You can apply directly to laboratory facilities in your area, contact your local employment office, or check your local newspaper's help wanted ads. If you complete a training program, placement assistance is often available to graduates.

ADVANCEMENT

Some histologic technicians become laboratory supervisors. Others specialize in certain areas of histotechnology such as orthopedic implants or diseases of the lungs. Technicians who have more education and experience are more likely to be promoted. In the future, an associate's degree is likely to become the standard requirement for entering the field and being promoted. Returning to school and earning a bachelor's degree will also provide opportunities for advancement into other medical or business fields.

EARNINGS

According to the U.S. Department of Labor, median earnings of clinical laboratory technicians were $27,540 in 2000. The lowest 10 percent earned less than $18,550, and the highest 10 percent earned more than $42,370 a year. These figures include a broad spectrum of laboratory jobs.

According to the American Society of Clinical Pathology, the national salary average for histologic technicians ranged from $24,960 to $35,984 in 2000. Wages are generally higher in the Northeast and Western regions of the United States.

In general, geographic location, experience, level of education, type of employer, and work performed determine the salary range for histologic technicians. Education, certification, experience, and specialization can increase earnings for histologic technicians.

Benefits such as vacation time, sick leave, health insurance, and other fringe benefits vary by employer, but are usually consistent with other full-time health care workers.

WORK ENVIRONMENT

Histologic technicians work in laboratories that are well ventilated. Most of the tissue processors that they use are enclosed, minimizing inhalation of odors and chemical fumes. Histologic technicians occasionally work with hazardous chemicals but wear protective clothing and carefully monitor exposure levels. They also face the risk of contact with disease through tissue samples. However, the steps involved in preparing specimens generally kill any living organisms.

Some histologic technicians may spend a great deal of time standing or sitting in one position and performing one type of operation, though most are able to rotate jobs. They must also deal with government regulations and spend time complying with required reports and organizing paperwork. Technicians who work for large laboratories or hospitals may be required to work rotating shifts, including weekends and holidays.

OUTLOOK

Employment for clinical laboratory workers is expected to grow about as fast as the average for all occupations through 2010, according to the *Occupational Outlook Handbook*. Advances in technology will have both positive and negative effects on employment in this career. The development of new tests and procedures is expected to increase opportunities, but at the same time many tests are being simplified so that health care professionals and patients can perform them themselves.

FOR MORE INFORMATION

For information on histologic technician careers, accredited schools, and employment opportunities, contact the following organizations:

American Medical Association
515 North State Street
Chicago, IL 60610
Tel: 312-464-5000
http://www.ama-assn.org

American Society of Clinical Pathology
Board of Registry
2100 West Harrison Street
Chicago, IL 60612
Tel: 312-738-1336
Email: info@ascp.org
http://www.ascp.org

National Accrediting Agency for Clinical Laboratory Sciences
8410 West Bryn Mawr Avenue, Suite 670
Chicago, IL 60631
Tel: 773-714-8880
Email: info@naacls.org
http://www.naacls.org

For career information and a list of schools of histotechnology, contact
National Society for Histotechnology
4201 Northview Drive, Suite 502
Bowie, MD 20716-2604
Tel: 301-262-6221
Email: histo@nsh.org
http://www.nsh.org

Medical Laboratory Technicians

QUICK FACTS

School Subjects
Biology
Chemistry

Personal Skills
Following instructions
Technical/scientific

Work Environment
Primarily indoors
Primarily one location

Minimum Education Level
Some postsecondary training

Salary Range
$18,550 to $27,540 to
$55,560+

Certification or Licensing
Required by certain states

Outlook
About as fast as the average

DOT
078

GOE
02.04.02

NOC
3212

O*NET-SOC
29-2012.00

OVERVIEW

Medical laboratory technicians perform routine tests in medical laboratories. These tests help physicians and other professional medical personnel diagnose and treat disease. Technicians prepare samples of body tissue; perform laboratory tests, such as urinalysis and blood counts; and make chemical and biological analyses of cells, tissue, blood, or other body specimens. They usually work under the supervision of a medical technologist or a laboratory director. Medical laboratory technicians may work in many fields, or specialize in one specific medical area, such as cytology (the study of cells), hematology (blood), serology (body fluids), or histology (body tissue). There are about 295,000 medical laboratory technologists and technicians employed in the United States.

HISTORY

Medical laboratory technology shares many important milestones with the history of medicine itself. For instance, both fields can claim as their founder Aristotle, the father of biology and physiology. Some significant achievements include Jan Swammerdam's discovery of red blood corpuscles in 1658, Anton van Leeuwenhoek's observation of microorganisms through the microscope during the latter part of the 17th century, and the discoveries of Robert Koch and Louis Pasteur in bacteriology in the 1870s.

The valuable information gained through these efforts showed medical professionals many possibilities for therapy, especially in the medical specialties of bacteriology (the study of microorganisms in the human body), cytology, histology, and hematology. The growth of these medical specialties created a steadily increasing need for laboratory personnel.

Because of the great medical advances of the 20th century, physicians are even more dependent on laboratory procedures and personnel for assistance in diagnosing and treating disease. In the early part of this century, individual physicians often taught their assistants how to perform some of the laboratory procedures frequently employed in their practices. Because the quality of work done by these technicians varied considerably, many physicians and medical educators became concerned with the problem of ensuring that assistants did the highest quality work possible. In 1936, one of the first attempts was made to standardize the training programs for the preparation of skilled assistants—in that case, the training of medical technologists. Since then, the National Accrediting Agency for Clinical Laboratory Sciences, in association with the Committee on Allied Health Education and Accreditation of the American Medical Association (CAHEA), has instituted standards of training for medical laboratory technicians. CAHEA has accredited more than 100 educational programs offered in community, junior, and technical colleges for the training of medical laboratory technicians, and other accrediting agencies have also entered the field. For example, the Accrediting Bureau of Health Education Schools accredits education programs for medical laboratory technicians and medical assistants. In addition, CAHEA and other agencies have accredited dozens of other programs for students willing to concentrate their studies in a medical laboratory specialty such as cytology, histology, or blood bank technology.

THE JOB

Medical laboratory technicians may be generalists in the field of laboratory technology; that is, they may be trained to carry out many different kinds of medical laboratory work. Alternatively, they may specialize in one type of medical laboratory work, such as cytology, hematology, blood bank technology, serology, or histology. The following paragraphs describe the work of generalists and those in the specialty fields of cytology, histology, and blood bank technology.

Medical laboratory technicians who work as generalists perform a wide variety of tests and laboratory procedures in chemistry, hematology (the study of blood, especially on the cellular level), urinalysis, blood banking, serology (the study and identification of antibodies found in the blood), and microbiology. By performing these tests and procedures, they help to develop vital data on the blood, tissues, and fluids of the human body. Physicians, surgeons, pathologists, and other medical personnel then use this data to diagnose and treat patients.

The tests and procedures that these technicians perform are more complex than the routine duties assigned to laboratory assistants, but do not require specialized knowledge like those performed by more highly trained medical technologists. In general, medical laboratory technicians work with only limited supervision. This means that while the tests they perform may have well-established procedures, the technicians themselves must exercise independent judgment. For instance, they must be able to discriminate between very similar colors or shapes, correct their own errors using established strategies, and monitor ongoing quality control measures.

To carry out these responsibilities, medical laboratory technicians need a sound knowledge of specific techniques and instruments and must be able to recognize factors that potentially influence both the procedures they use and the results they obtain.

In their work, medical laboratory technicians frequently handle test tubes and other glassware and use precision equipment, such as microscopes and automated blood analyzers. (Blood analyzers determine the levels of certain blood components like cholesterol, sugar, and hemoglobin.) Technicians also are often responsible for making sure machines are functioning and supplies are adequately stocked.

Medical laboratory technicians who specialize in cytology are usually referred to as *cytotechnicians*. Cytotechnicians prepare and stain body cell samplings using special dyes that accentuate the delicate patterns of the cytoplasm, and structures such as the nucleus. Mounted on slides, the various features of the specimen then stand out brightly under a microscope. Using microscopes that magnify cells perhaps 1,000 times, cytotechnicians screen out normal samplings and set aside those with minute irregularities (in cell size, shape, and color) for further study by a pathologist.

Medical laboratory technicians specializing in histology are usually referred to as *histologic technicians* or *tissue technicians*. Histology is the study of the structure and chemical composition of the tissues, and histologic technicians are mainly concerned with detecting tissue abnormalities and assisting in determining appropriate treatments for the disease conditions associated with the abnormalities. For more information, see the article "Histologic Technicians."

Medical laboratory technicians who specialize in blood bank technology perform a wide variety of routine tests related to running blood banks, offering transfusion services, and investigating blood diseases and reactions to transfusions. Examples of tasks frequently performed by medical laboratory technicians specializing in this field include donor screening, determining blood types, performing tests of patients' blood counts, and assisting physicians in the care of patients with blood-related problems.

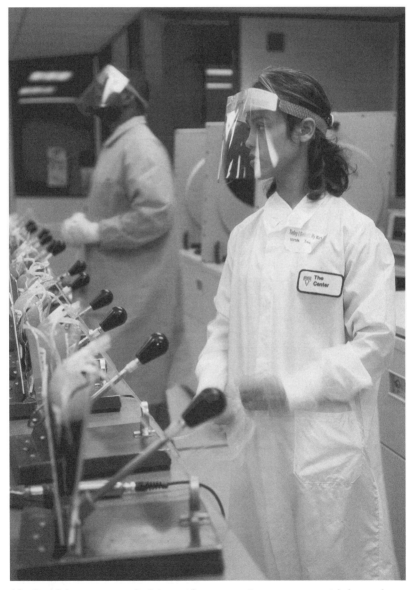

Medical laboratory technicians often come into contact with hazardous materials, thus they frequently wear protective clothing. *(Corbis)*

Most positions of responsibility in blood bank technology are held by certified specialists in blood bank technology. To become certified in this field, a person needs a bachelor's degree and an additional year of training, which helps technicians become involved with research projects, teaching other health care workers, and supervising other employees.

REQUIREMENTS

High School

To be hired as a medical laboratory technician, you must have a high school diploma and one or two years of postsecondary training. No specific kind of high school training is required; however, you must be able to meet the admissions requirements of institutions offering post-high-school training. In general, courses in biology, chemistry, mathematics, English, and computer science will be most helpful in a career as a medical laboratory technician.

Postsecondary Training

After high school, prospective technicians enroll in one- or two-year training programs accredited by the American Medical Association's Committee on Allied Health Education and Accreditation or the Accrediting Bureau of Health Education Schools. One-year programs include both classroom work and practical laboratory training and focus on areas such as medical ethics and conduct, medical terminology, basic laboratory solutions and media, manipulation of cytological and histological specimens, blood collecting techniques, and introductions to basic hematology, serology, blood banking, and urinalysis.

To earn an associate's degree, you must complete a two-year post-high school program. Like certificate programs, associate's degree programs include classroom instruction and practical training. Courses are taught both on campus and in local hospitals. On-campus courses focus on general knowledge and basic skills in laboratory testing associated with hematology, serology, chemistry, microbiology, and other pertinent biological and medical areas. The clinical training program focuses on basic principles and skills required in medical diagnostic laboratory testing.

Certification or Licensing

Students who have earned an associate's degree are eligible for certification from several different agencies. They may become a certified medical laboratory technician (MLT) by the Board of Registry of the American Society of Clinical Pathology or the American Medical Technologists. In addition, the National Credentialing Agency for

Laboratory Personnel offers certification for clinical laboratory technicians (CLTs).

Prospective medical laboratory technicians who think they might want to specialize in cytology or blood bank technology should definitely consider the two-year program, which will best prepare them for the additional education they may need later.

In addition to completing the educational programs described above, prospective technicians need to pass an examination after graduation to receive certification. In some states, this certificate is all that is required for employment. In other states, state licensure is also required. School officials are the best source of information regarding state requirements.

Other Requirements

Besides fulfilling the academic requirements, medical laboratory technicians must have good manual dexterity, normal color vision, the ability to follow orders, and a tolerance for working under pressure.

EXPLORING

It is difficult for people interested in a career in medical laboratory technology to gain any direct experience through part-time employment. There are some other ways, however, to learn more about this career on a firsthand basis. Perhaps the best way is to arrange a visit to a hospital, blood bank, or commercial medical laboratory to see technicians at work at their jobs. Another way to learn about this kind of work in general, and about the training required in particular, is to visit an accredited school of medical laboratory technology to discuss career plans with the admissions counselor at the school. You can also write to the sources listed at the end of this article for more reading material on medical laboratory technology. Finally, students should remember that high school science courses with laboratory sections provide exposure to some of the kinds of work that medical laboratory technicians do.

EMPLOYERS

Medical laboratory technicians are employed where physicians work, such as in hospitals, clinics, blood blanks, and commercial medical laboratories.

STARTING OUT

Graduates of medical laboratory technology schools usually receive assistance from faculty and school placement services to find their first jobs. Hospitals, laboratories, and other facilities employing medical laboratory technicians may notify local schools of job openings. Often the hospital or laboratory at which you receive your practical training will offer full-time employment after graduation. Positions may also be secured using the various registries of certified medical laboratory workers. Newspaper job advertisements and commercial placement agencies are other sources of help in locating employment.

ADVANCEMENT

Medical laboratory technicians often advance by returning to school to earn a bachelor's degree. This can lead to positions as medical technologists, histological technologists, cytotechnologists, or specialists in blood bank technology.

Other technicians advance by gaining more responsibility while retaining the title of technician. For instance, with experience, these workers can advance to supervisory positions or other positions assigning work to be done by other medical laboratory workers. Medical laboratory technicians may also advance by training to do very specialized or complex laboratory or research work.

EARNINGS

Salaries of medical laboratory technicians vary according to employer and geographical area. According to salary.com, medical laboratory technicians earned a median base salary of $31,664 in May 2001. Fifty percent of workers in this field earn between $28,794 and $34,674 annually. The U.S. Department of Labor reports that median annual earnings of medical and clinical laboratory technicians were $27,540 in 2000. The lowest 10 percent earned less than $18,550, and the highest 10 percent earned more than $42,370.

Medical laboratory technicians who go on to earn their bachelor's degrees and certification as medical technologists can expect an increase in annual earnings. According to the U.S. Department of Labor, median annual earnings of medical and clinical laboratory technologists were $40,510 in 2000. Salaries ranged from less than $29,240 to more than $55,560.

Most medical laboratory technicians receive paid vacations and holidays, sick leave, health insurance, and retirement benefits.

WORK ENVIRONMENT

Medical laboratory technicians work in clean, well lighted, climate-controlled settings. There may, however, be unpleasant odors and some infectious materials involved in the work. In general, there are few hazards associated with these odors and materials as long as proper methods of sterilization and handling of specimens, materials, and equipment are used.

Medical laboratory technicians often spend much of their days standing or sitting on stools. A 40-hour, five-day week is normal, although those working in hospitals can expect some evening and weekend work.

Medical laboratory technicians derive satisfaction from knowing their work is very important to patients and their physicians. Although the work involves new patient samples, it also involves some very repetitive tasks that some people may find trying. Additionally, the work must often be done under time pressure, even though it is often very painstaking.

Another factor that aspiring medical laboratory technicians should keep in mind is that advancement opportunities are limited, although they do exist. To maximize their chances for advancement, medical laboratory technicians must consider getting additional training.

OUTLOOK

The U.S. Department of Labor predicts job growth for medical laboratory technicians to be about as fast as the average through 2010. Competition for jobs, however, may be strong. One reason for this increased competition is the overall national effort to control health care costs. Hospitals, where most medical laboratory technicians are employed, will seek to control costs in part through cutting down on the amount of laboratory testing they do and, consequently, the personnel they require.

Despite such cutbacks, though, the overall amount of medical laboratory testing will probably increase, as much of medical practice today relies on high-quality laboratory testing. However, because of the increased use of automation, this increase in laboratory testing probably will not lead to an equivalent growth in employment.

One other technological factor that will influence employment in this field is the development of laboratory-testing equipment that is easier to use. This means that some testing that formerly had to be done in hospitals or commercial laboratories can now be done in physicians' offices. This development may serve to slow growth in medical laboratory employment; however, it may increase the number of technicians hired by medical groups and clinics. In addition, equipment that is easier to use may also lead to technicians being able to do more kinds of testing, including some tests that used to be done only by medical technologists.

Despite these moderate growth projections, aspiring technicians should keep in mind that medical laboratory testing is an absolutely essential element in today's medicine. For well-trained technicians who are flexible in accepting responsibilities and willing to continue their education throughout their careers, employment opportunities should remain good.

FOR MORE INFORMATION

For information on careers, certification, and continuing education, contact the following organizations:

American Medical Association
515 North State Street
Chicago, IL 60610
Tel: 312-464-5000
http://www.ama-assn.org

American Medical Technologists
710 Higgins Road
Park Ridge, IL 60068-5765
Tel: 847-823-5169
Email: mail@amt1.com
http://www.amt1.com

American Society for Clinical Laboratory Science
6701 Democracy Boulevard, Suite 300
Bethesda, MD 20817
Tel: 301-657-2768
http://www.ascls.org

American Association of Bioanalysts
917 Locust Street, Suite 1100
St. Louis, MO 63101-1419
Tel: 314-241-1445
Email: aab@aab.org
http://www.aab.org

National Credentialing Agency for Laboratory Personnel
PO Box 15945-289
Lenexa, KS 66285
Tel: 913-438-5110, ext. 647
Email: nca-info@goamp.com
http://www.nca-info.org

Medical Record Technicians

OVERVIEW

In any hospital, clinic, or other health care facility, permanent records are created and maintained for all the patients. Each patient's medical record describes in detail his or her condition over time. Entries include illness and injuries, operations, treatments, outpatient visits, and the progress of hospital stays. *Medical record technicians* compile, code, and maintain these records. They also tabulate and analyze data from groups of records in order to assemble reports. They review records for completeness and accuracy; assign codes to the diseases, operations, diagnoses, and treatments according to detailed standardized classification systems; and post the codes on the medical record. They transcribe medical reports; maintain indices of patients, diseases, operations, and other categories of information; compile patient census data; and file records. In addition, they may direct the day-to-day operations of the medical records department. They maintain the flow of records and reports to and from other departments, and sometimes assist medical staff in special studies or research that draws on information in the records. There are approximately 136,000 medical record technicians employed in the United States.

HISTORY

Prior to the 20th and 21st centuries, medical records mostly helped practitioners retain and learn as much as possible from their own experience. Because there was little centralization or standardization of this information, it was difficult to organize and share the knowledge that resulted from studying many instances of similar cases.

By the early 1900s, medical record keeping was changing, along with many other aspects of health care. Medicine was more sophisticated, scientific, and successful in helping patients. Hospitals were increasingly becoming accepted as the conventional place for middle-class patients to go for care, and as a result, hospitals became more numerous and better organized. As hospitals grew larger and served more patients, the volume of patient records increased proportionately. With medical record keeping becoming more important and time consuming, it was most efficient and sensible to centralize it within the hospital. Distinguished committees representing the medical profession also encouraged standardized record-keeping procedures.

By the 1920s, many hospitals in the United States had central libraries of patient information and hired employees specifically to keep these records in good order. As time passed, these employees' tasks became more complicated. The employees responsible for this work, who used to be called medical record librarians, eventually became differentiated into two basic professional categories: medical record administrators and medical record technicians. In 1953, the first formal training programs for medical record technicians started up in hospital schools and junior colleges.

In recent years, the computerization of records, the growing importance of privacy and freedom of information issues, and the changing requirements of insurance carriers have all had major impacts on the field of medical records technology. These areas will undoubtedly continue to reshape the field in future years.

THE JOB

A patient's medical record consists of all relevant information and observations from any health care workers who have dealt with the patient. The records may contain, for example, several diagnoses, X-ray and laboratory reports, electrocardiogram tracings, test results, and drugs prescribed. This summary of the patient's medical history is very important to the physician in making speedy and correct decisions about care. Later, information from the record is often needed in authenticating legal forms and insurance claims. The medical record documents the adequacy and appropriateness of the care received by the patient and is the basis of any investigation when the care is questioned in any way.

Patterns and trends can be traced when data from many records are considered together. These types of statistical reports are used by many different groups. Hospital administrators, scientists, public health agencies, accrediting and licensing bodies, people who evaluate the effectiveness of current programs or plan future ones, and medical reimbursement organizations are examples of some groups that rely on health care statistics. Medical records can provide the data to show whether a new treatment or medication really works, the relative effectiveness of alternative treatments or medications, or patterns that yield clues about the causes or methods of preventing certain kinds of disease.

Medical record technicians are involved in the routine preparation, handling, and safeguarding of individual records as well as the statistical information extracted from groups of records. Their specific tasks and the scope of their responsibilities depend a great deal on the size and type of the employing institution. In large organizations, there may be a number of technicians and other employees working with medical records. The technicians may serve as assistants to the medical record administrator as needed or may regularly specialize in some particular phase of the work done by the department. In small facilities, however, technicians often carry out the whole range of activities and may function fairly independently, perhaps bearing the full responsibility for all day-to-day operations of the department. A technician in a small facility may even be a department director. Sometimes technicians handle medical records and also spend part of their time helping out in the business or admitting office.

Whether they work in hospitals or other settings, medical record technicians must organize, transfer, analyze, preserve, and locate vast quantities of detailed information when needed. The sources of this information include physicians, nurses, laboratory workers, and other members of the health care team.

In a hospital, a patient's cumulative record goes to the medical record department at the end of the hospital stay. A technician checks over the information in the file to be sure that all the essential reports and data are included and appear accurate. Certain specific items must be supplied in any record, such as signatures, dates, the patient's physical and social history, the results of physical examinations, provisional and final diagnoses, periodic progress notes on the patient's condition during the hospital stay, medications prescribed and administered, therapeutic treatments, surgical procedures, and an assessment of the outcome or the condition at the time of discharge. If any item is missing, the technician sends the record to the person who is responsible for supplying the information. After all necessary information has been received and the record has passed the review, it is considered the official document describing the patient's case.

The record is then passed to a *medical record coder*. Coders are responsible for assigning a numeric code to every diagnosis and procedure listed in a patient's file. Most hospitals in the United States use a nationally accepted system for coding. The lists of diseases, procedures, and conditions are published in classification manuals that medical records personnel refer to frequently. By reducing information in different forms to a single consistent coding system, the data contained in the record is rendered much easier to handle, tabulate, and analyze. It can be indexed under any suitable heading, such as by patient, disease, type of surgery, physician attending the case, and so forth. Cross-indexing is likely to be an important part of the medical record technician's job. Because the same coding systems are used nearly everywhere in the United States, the data may be used not only by people working inside the hospital, but may also be submitted to one of the various programs that pool information obtained from many institutions.

After the information on the medical record has been coded, technicians may use a packaged computer program to assign the patient to one of several hundred diagnosis-related groupings, or DRGs. The DRG for the patient's stay determines the amount of money the hospital will receive if the patient is covered by Medicare or one of the other insurance programs that base their reimbursement on DRGs.

Because information in medical records is used to determine how much hospitals will be paid for patient care, the accuracy of the work done by medical records personnel is vital. A coding error could cause the hospital or patient to lose money.

Another vital part of the job concerns filing. Regardless of how accurately and completely information is gathered and stored, it is worthless unless it can be retrieved promptly. If paper records are kept, technicians are usually responsible for preparing records for storage, filing them, and getting them out of storage when needed. In some organizations, technicians supervise other personnel who carry out these tasks.

In many health care facilities, computers, rather than paper, are used for nearly all the medical record keeping. In such cases, medical and nursing staff make notes on an electronic chart. They enter patient-care information into computer files, and medical record technicians access the information using their own terminals. Computers have greatly simplified many traditional routine tasks of the medical records department, such as generating daily hospital census figures, tabulating data for research purposes, and updating special registries of certain types of health problems, such as cancer and stroke.

In the past, some medical records that were originally on paper were later photographed and stored on microfilm, particularly after they were a year or two old. Medical record technicians may be responsible for retrieving and maintaining those films. It is not unusual for a health care institution to have a combination of paper and microfilm files as well as computerized record storage, reflecting the evolution of technology for storing information.

Confidentiality and privacy laws have a major bearing on the medical records field. The laws vary in different states for different types of data, but in all cases, maintaining the confidentiality of individual records is of major concern to medical records workers. All individual records must be in secure storage but also be available for retrieval and specified kinds of properly authorized use. Technicians may be responsible for retrieving and releasing this information. They may prepare records to be released in response to a patient's written authorization, a subpoena, or a court order. This requires special knowledge of legal statutes and often requires consultation with attorneys, judges, insurance agents, and other parties with legitimate rights to access information about a person's health and medical treatment.

Medical record technicians may participate in the quality assurance, risk management, and utilization review activities of a health care facility. In these cases, they may serve as *data abstractors* and *data analysts,* reviewing records against established standards to ensure quality of care. They may also prepare statistical reports for the medical or administrative staff that reviews appropriateness of care.

With more specialized training, medical record technicians may participate in medical research activities by maintaining special records, called registries, related to such areas as cancer, heart disease, transplants, or adverse outcomes of pregnancies. In some cases, they are required to abstract and code information from records of patients with certain medical conditions. These technicians also may prepare statistical reports and trend analyses for the use of medical researchers.

REQUIREMENTS

High School

If you are contemplating a career in medical records, you should take as many high school English classes as possible, because technicians need both written and verbal communication skills to prepare reports and communicate with other health care personnel. Basic math or business math is very desirable because statistical skills are important in some job functions. Biology courses will help to familiarize yourself with the terminology that medical record technicians use. Other science courses, computer training, typing, and office procedures are also helpful.

Postsecondary Training

Most employers prefer to hire medical record technicians who have completed a two-year associate's degree program accredited by the American Medical Association's Commission on Accreditation of Allied Health Professions and the American Health Information Management Association (AHIMA). There are 177 of these accredited programs available throughout the United States, mostly offered in junior and community colleges. They usually include classroom instruction in such subjects as anatomy, physiology, medical terminology, medical record science, word processing, medical aspects of record keeping, statistics, computers in health care, personnel supervision, business management, English, and office skills.

In addition to classroom instruction, the student gains supervised clinical experience in the medical records departments of local health care facilities. This provides students with practical experience in performing many of the functions learned in the classroom and the opportunity to interact with health care professionals.

An alternative educational method is open to individuals with experience in certain related activities. It requires completion of an independent study program offered by the AHIMA. Students in this program must successfully complete a lesson series and clinical experience internship in a health care institution. They must also earn 30 semester hours of credit in prescribed subjects at a college or university.

Certification or Licensing

Medical record technicians who have completed an accredited training program are eligible to take a national qualifying examination to earn the credential of registered health information technician (RHIT). Most health care institutions prefer to hire individuals with an RHIT credential as this shows the person meets the AHIMA standards for qualified health professionals.

Other Requirements

Medical records are extremely detailed and precise. Sloppy work could have serious consequences in terms of payment to the hospital or physician, validity of the patient records for later use, and validity of research based on data from medical records. Therefore, a prospective technician must have the capacity to do consistently reliable and accurate work. Records must be completed and maintained with care and attention to detail. You may be the only person who checks the entire record, and you must understand the responsibility that accompanies this task.

In many medical record departments, the workload is very heavy, and you must be well organized and efficient in order to stay on top of the job. You must be able to complete your work accurately, in spite of interruptions, such as phone calls and requests for assistance. You also need to be discreet, as you will deal with records that are private and sometimes sensitive.

Computer skills also are essential, and some experience in transcribing dictated reports may be useful.

EXPLORING

To learn more about this and other medical careers, you may be able to find summer, part-time, or volunteer work in a hospital or other health care facility. Sometimes such jobs are available in the medical records area of an organization. You may also be able to arrange to talk with someone working as a medical record technician or administrator. Faculty and counselors at schools that offer medical record technician training programs may also be good sources of information. You also can learn more about this profession by reading journals and other literature available at a public library.

EMPLOYERS

Although most medical record technicians work in hospitals, many work in other health care settings, including health maintenance organizations (HMOs), industrial clinics, skilled nursing facilities, rehabilitation centers, large group medical practices, ambulatory care centers, and state and local government health agencies. Technicians also work for computer firms, consulting firms, and government agencies. Records are maintained in all these facilities, although record-keeping procedures vary.

Not all medical record technicians are employed in a single health care facility; some serve as consultants to several small facilities. Other technicians do not work in health care settings at all. They may be employed by health and property liability insurance companies to collect and review information on medical claims. A few are self-employed, providing medical transcription services.

STARTING OUT

Most successful medical record technicians are graduates of two-year accredited programs. Graduates of these programs should check with their schools' placement offices for job leads. Those who have taken the accrediting exam and have become certified can use the AHIMA's resume referral service.

You may also apply directly to the personnel departments of hospitals, nursing homes, outpatient clinics, and surgery centers. Many job openings are also listed in the classified advertising sections of local newspapers and with private and public employment agencies.

ADVANCEMENT

Medical record technicians may be able to achieve some advancement and salary increase without additional training simply by taking on greater responsibility in their job function. With experience, you may move to supervisory or department head positions, depending on the type and structure of the employing organization. Another means of advancing is through specialization in a certain area of the job. Some technicians specialize in coding, particularly Medicare coding or tumor registry. With a broad range of experience, you may be able to become an independent consultant. Generally, technicians with an associate's degree and the RHIT designation are most likely to advance.

More assured job advancement and salary increase come with the completion of a bachelor's degree in medical record administration. The bachelor's degree, along with AHIMA accreditation, makes the technician eligible for a supervisory position, such as department director. Because of a general shortage of medical record administrators, hospitals often assist technicians who are working toward a bachelor's degree by providing flexible scheduling and financial aid or tuition reimbursement.

EARNINGS

The salaries of medical record technicians are greatly influenced by the location, size, and type of employing institution, as well as the technician's training and experience. According to the AHIMA, beginning technicians with an associate's degree can earn between $20,000 to $30,000 annually. Those who have earned a bachelor's degree can expect to earn between $30,000 and $50,000 a year.

The AHIMA's 2001 membership profile reports that the majority of its members designated coding professionals earned between

$30,000 and $40,000. However, with higher educational achievement comes higher salaries. According to the same membership profile, 27 percent of those with a baccalaureate degree and 59 percent of those who have earned a master's degree earn $50,000 or more annually.

According to the Bureau of Labor Statistics, the median annual earnings of medical records and health information technicians were $23,530 in 2001. Salaries ranged from less than $16,220 to more than $37,030.

In general, medical record technicians working in large urban hospitals make the most money, and those in rural areas make the least. Like most hospital employees, medical record technicians usually receive paid vacations and holidays, life and health insurance, and retirement benefits.

WORK ENVIRONMENT

Medical records departments are usually pleasantly clean, well-lit, and air-conditioned areas. Sometimes, however, paper or microfilm records are kept in cramped, out-of-the-way quarters. Although the work requires thorough and careful attention to detail, there may be a constant bustle of activity in the technician's work area, which can be disruptive. The job is likely to involve frequent routine contact with nurses, physicians, hospital administrators, other health care professionals, attorneys, and insurance agents. On occasion, individuals with whom the technicians may interact with are demanding or difficult. In such cases, technicians may find that the job carries a high level of frustration.

A 40-hour workweek is the norm, but because hospitals operate on a 24-hour basis, the job may regularly include night or weekend hours. Part-time work is sometimes available.

The work is extremely detailed and may be tedious. Some technicians spend the majority of their day sitting at a desk, working on a computer. Others may spend hours filing paper records or retrieving them from storage.

In many hospital settings, the medical record technician experiences pressure caused by a heavy workload. As the demands for health care cost containment and productivity increase, medical record technicians may be required to produce a significantly greater volume of high-quality work in shorter periods of time.

Nonetheless, the knowledge that their work is significant for patients and medical research can be personally very satisfying for medical record technicians.

OUTLOOK

Employment prospects through 2010 are excellent. The U.S. Department of Labor predicts that employment in this field will grow by 54.1 percent between 2000 and 2010. The demand for well-trained medical record technicians will grow rapidly and will continue to exceed the supply. This is related to the health care needs of a population that is both growing and aging and the trend toward more technologically sophisticated medicine and greater use of diagnostic procedures. It is also related to the increased requirements of regulatory bodies that scrutinize both costs and quality of care of health care providers. Because of the fear of medical malpractice lawsuits, doctors and other health care providers are documenting their diagnoses and treatments in greater detail. Also, because of the high cost of health care, insurance companies, government agencies, and courts are examining medical records with a more critical eye. These factors combine to ensure a healthy job outlook for medical record technicians.

Technicians with associate's degrees and RHIT status will have the best prospects, and the importance of such qualifications is likely to increase.

FOR MORE INFORMATION

For information on careers in health information management and accreditation, contact
American Health Information Management Association
233 North Michigan Avenue, Suite 2150
Chicago, IL 60601-5800
Tel: 312-233-1100
Email: info@ahima.org
http://www.ahima.org

For a list of schools offering accredited programs in health information management, contact
Commission on Accreditation of Allied Health Education
  Programs
35 East Wacker Drive, Suite 1970
Chicago, IL 60601-2208
Tel: 312-553-9355
Email: caahep@caahep.org
http://www.caahep.org

Medical Technologists

OVERVIEW

Medical technologists, also called *clinical laboratory technologists*, are health professionals whose jobs include many health care roles. They perform laboratory tests essential to the detection, diagnosis, and treatment of disease. They work under the direction of laboratory managers and pathologists.

HISTORY

The history of clinical laboratory work is intertwined with the development of medicine itself. By the end of the 19th century, bacteriology and other medical specialties had developed rapidly, creating demand for full-time laboratory personnel. In the early part of the 20th century, many physicians taught their assistants how to perform some of the laboratory procedures frequently used in their practice. The quality of the work done by these assistants varied greatly, and in the 1930s, an attempt was made to standardize training programs then available for the preparation of medical technologists. Professional societies for these technologists were established because of their important role in medical advancement. Medical and laboratory technologists have become integral to the health care system.

QUICK FACTS

School Subjects
Biology
Chemistry

Personal Skills
Helping/teaching
Technical/scientific

Work Environment
Primarily indoors
Primarily one location

Minimum Education Level
Bachelor's degree

Salary Range
$29,120 to $40,510 to $63,024

Certification or Licensing
Recommended (certification)
Required by certain states (licensing)

Outlook
About as fast as the average

DOT
078

GOE
02.04.02

NOC
3219

O*NET-SOC
29-2011.00

THE JOB

Medical technologists perform laboratory tests to help physicians detect, diagnose, and treat diseases. The work of medical technologists is generally done under the supervision of a senior medical technologist, a clinical laboratory supervisor, or a physician who has specialized in diagnosing the causes and nature of disease.

Technologists in clinical practice ensure the quality of laboratory tests done for diagnosis. They may be responsible for interpreting the data and results and reporting their findings to the attending physicians. Many also assist attending physicians in correlating test results with clinical data and recommend tests and test sequences. Medical technologists may also have management and supervisory tasks, including serving as laboratory manager, supervisor of lab sections, and staff supervisor over other technologists and laboratory personnel.

The specific tasks performed by medical technologists are determined by the kind of setting in which they work. Technologists employed by small laboratories conduct many kinds of tests, such as blood counts, urinalyses, and skin tests. They use microscopes to examine body fluids and tissue samples to determine the presence of bacteria, fungi, or other organisms. They sometimes prepare slides from sample tissues and body cells to ascertain, for example, whether an individual has developed cancer. Depending on the laboratory facilities and needs, they may be responsible for operating highly sophisticated medical instruments and machines. They conduct research and maintain and make minor repairs to the instruments and equipment used in testing. Medical technologists employed in large laboratories are generally specialists.

Medical technology specialists normally have advanced degrees in their area of expertise. They are capable of handling sophisticated equipment and tests because of their education and training. They may be responsible for ordering, purchasing, maintaining, and repairing specialized equipment and instruments required for the laboratory tests. They design new laboratory procedures and establish or continue training and education of other employees in laboratory procedures and skills.

Clinical laboratory directors oversee the laboratory or the laboratory department. They usually hold an M.D., D.O., or Ph.D. They are responsible for the supervision of the technologists on the staff and for the quality of the work done. They may be in charge of sustaining the budget and determining the financial needs and responsibilities of the lab. They will assign duties, hire and fire staff, and establish work rules and standards.

Clinical laboratory supervisors, or *medical technology supervisors,* are the managers of the staff on a day-to-day basis. The supervisor assigns work schedules and assignments, reviews work and lab results, and may assist in training and continued education of the staff. The supervisor may also continue performing duties of the medical technologist. The *chief medical technologist* supervises the work of the entire laboratory operations, assigns duties, and reviews the reports and analyses.

A *chemistry technologist,* or *biochemistry technologist,* tests specimens of blood, urine, gastric juices, and spinal fluid to detect the presence of chemicals, drugs, and poisons, as well as levels of substances made by the body, such as sugar, albumin, and acetone. This information may be used in the diagnosis of metabolic disease such as diabetes. Precise measurements are made with equipment maintained by the technologist.

A *microbiology technologist,* or *bacteriology technologist,* examines specimens for microorganisms, including viruses, fungi, parasites, and bacteria. It may be necessary to isolate and grow a specific organism to make a better identification for diagnosis. Treatment of a condition may depend on the results of testing various ways of dealing with the organism itself, before the patient can be treated.

REQUIREMENTS

High School

If you are interested in this career, take college preparatory classes while you are in high school. Science courses, especially those involving laboratory work, such as biology and chemistry, will be particularly helpful. Be sure to take math classes, including algebra and calculus, and computer science courses, which will aid you in preparing for working with calculations and technology. Round out your education with humanities classes, including English. English courses will give you the opportunity to develop your research and report writing skills.

Postsecondary Training

After you finish high school, your next step on the path to becoming a medical technologist is to get a bachelor's degree. A number of colleges and universities offer degrees in medical technology and clinical laboratory science. The typical course of study will involve a "preprofessional" phase lasting two or three years during which you take classes such as chemistry, biology, math, physiology, psychology, English, and statistics. Following this, you enter a professional phase that is specialized for medical technologists. During this portion of your studies, generally lasting 12 months, you will take classes, such as immunohematology, clinical chemistry, and virology, as well as get hands-on experience working at the medical center or hospital lab associated with your program. You may also be required or encouraged to take classes in management, business, and computer science to prepare you for work in a professional setting. The National Accrediting Agency for Clinical Laboratory Sciences (NAACLS) accredits medical technologist programs, and those who graduate from such programs are eligible to sit for certifying exams. Visit the NAACLS website to view a listing of schools across the country (http://www.naacls.org). Requirements for graduation may vary according to specialty.

Advanced work in medical technology leading to graduate degrees and subsequent employment in teaching and research positions is available at an increasing number of universities.

Certification or Licensing

Certification of medical technologists verifies that people in the profession have met the educational standards recognized by the certifying body. After meeting certain education and experience requirements and passing appropriate examinations, candidates may be certified as medical technologists (MTs) by the Board of Registry of the American Society of Clinical Pathology, the American Medical Technologists, or the American Association of Bioanalysts. Another option is to become a clinical laboratory scientist (CLS), offered by the National Credentialing Agency for Laboratory Personnel. Certification is highly recommended for those who wish to advance in this field; some employers will not hire technologists without certification.

Puerto Rico and some states require medical technologists to be licensed or registered. Because licensure requirements vary and because new licensing laws may be adopted in other states, you will need to check with your state's department of health or occupational licensing board for specific information about your area. Those in the profession predict that licensing will become more common as insurance companies involve the evaluation of laboratory certification (which affects the diagnoses of patients) in the cost of insurance to doctors and clinics.

Other Requirements

Because of the nature of the work, students interested in careers in medical technology should possess the following characteristics: accuracy, patience, and the ability to work under pressure. Other essential characteristics are manual dexterity and good eyesight (with or without glasses). Because the medical technologist must survive a rigorous training program, above-average scholastic aptitude is also necessary.

EXPLORING

You can learn about the health care field and hospital environments by doing volunteer work at a local hospital or medical facility. Although you probably won't be in the lab analyzing samples, you will be able to observe the workings of the institution and may meet professionals willing to talk to you about their work. You can also ask your school counselor or science teacher to set up a career day during which a medical technologist would be invited to talk to interested students. Another possibility is to contact a local hospital or clinic and set up your own informational interview with a technologist. If you live in an area near an NAACLS-approved medical technologist program, visit the school and discuss career plans with an admissions counselor there. You should also contact sources listed at the end of this article for more reading material on medical technology.

EMPLOYERS

According to the U.S. Department of Labor, about half of all medical technologists work in hospitals. Other employers include clinics, physicians' offices, pharmaceutical labs, public health agencies, and research institutions. Some technologists work in Department of Veterans Affairs hospitals and blood banks as well as in the armed forces and the U.S. public health service.

Medical technologists may concentrate on such areas as research, education, health policy development (particularly in government organizations), veterinary science, public health and epidemiology study and application, or diagnostic equipment research and development.

STARTING OUT

Graduates of schools of medical technology may receive assistance from placement services at the schools in securing their first jobs. Hospitals, laboratories, and other companies employing medical technologists often get in touch with these placement offices and notify them of job openings. Positions may also be secured with the assistance of various registries of medical technologists. Newspaper advertisements and commercial placement agencies are other sources of initial employment.

ADVANCEMENT

Advancement can be relatively rapid in the field of medical technology. With satisfactory experience, certification, and perhaps more training, a medical technologist may advance to a supervisory position. Specialization can also lead to advancement. A medical technologist who has gained expertise in a specialty area, such as cell marker technology, biogenetics, or product development, is likely to see an increase in salary, professional prestige, and responsibilities. Considerable experience is required for advancement to a position as chief medical technologist in a large hospital. Graduate training is necessary for advancement to positions in research and teaching.

Advancement prospects may be better in large hospitals or independent laboratories that have many departments.

EARNINGS

A 2000 wage and vacancy survey conducted by the American Society of Clinical Pathology's Board of Registry (BOR) found that medical technologists in beginning staff positions earned a median of $14 per hour (which translates into a yearly salary of $29,120 for full-time work). Those who had just moved into supervisor positions earned a median of $17 per hour ($35,360 per year). Medical technologists in manager positions had median earnings ranging from $21 per hour ($43,680 annually) to $30.30 per hour ($63,024 annually). Earnings varied within these categories based on such factors as employer, size of city, and location in the country. Those working in the far West, which included California, Oregon, Idaho, Montana, and New Mexico, among others, reported the highest earnings. Those who worked for private clinics, small hospitals, and in rural areas had the lowest earnings.

The U.S. Department of Labor reports that median annual earnings of medical laboratory technologists were $40,510 in 2000. Salaries ranged from less than $29,240, to more than $55,560.

Benefits vary by employer but typically include paid vacation time, sick leave, and health insurance.

WORK ENVIRONMENT

Medical laboratory personnel usually work a 35- to 40-hour week. Night or weekend duty is often required in hospitals. However, with the current staff shortage, overtime in some facilities has become common, with required amounts of overtime hours assigned to staff.

Medical technologists must exercise meticulous care in their work to avoid risk of exposure to diseases or contamination of a testing sample, requiring the retesting of the patient. Plastics have replaced glass, so risk of cuts from broken equipment is greatly reduced. Chemicals and their containers and usage have also improved with the advancement of technology, so chemical burns are rare. Lab workers must often work under pressure at painstaking tasks. Workloads can be heavy because of staff shortage in the workplace.

OUTLOOK

According to the U.S. Department of Labor, employment of clinical laboratory workers is expected to grow about as fast as the average through 2010. Because of a general shortage in hospital staffs, there will be a number of openings for new medical technologists wishing to work in hospital labs. Job opportunities should also be available at laboratories outside of hospitals.

A June 2001 article in the *New York Times* reported strong growth of medical laboratory companies due, in part, to scientists' progress in understanding the human genetic code. This new understanding has led to, and should continue to lead to, the development of numerous new diagnostic tests to be performed in laboratories. In addition, the 2000 wage and vacancy survey by the American Society of Clinical Pathologisty's BOR revealed that 66 percent of all labs with available positions were having difficulty filling these vacancies on at least one shift for medical technologist staff. Factors moderating growth in this field include insurance companies' unwillingness to pay for expensive lab tests and the development of tests that patients can administer on their own—both of which translate into less work for lab technologists. Overall, however, this remains a field with a good employment outlook.

FOR MORE INFORMATION

For information on careers, certification, and educational programs, contact the following organizations:
American Association for Clinical Chemistry
2101 L Street, NW, Suite 202
Washington, DC 20037-1558
Tel: 800-892-1400
Email: info@aacc.org
http://www.aacc.org

American Association of Bioanalysts
917 Locust Street, Suite 1100
St. Louis, MO 63101-1419
Tel: 314-241-1445
Email: aab@aab.org
http://www.aab.org

American Medical Technologists
710 Higgins Road
Park Ridge, IL 60068-5765
Tel: 847-823-5169
Email: mail@amt1.com
http://www.amt1.com

American Society for Clinical Laboratory Science
6701 Democracy Boulevard, Suite 300
Bethesda, MD 20817
Tel: 301-657-2768
Email: ascls@ascls.org
http://www.ascls.org

American Society for Clinical Pathology
2100 West Harrison Street
Chicago, IL 60612
Tel: 312-738-1336
Email: info@ascp.org
http://www.ascp.org

For information on accredited schools and the accrediting process, contact
National Accrediting Agency for Clinical Laboratory Sciences
8410 West Bryn Mawr Avenue, Suite 670
Chicago, IL 60631
Tel: 773-714-8880
Email: info@naacls.org
http://www.naacls.org

For certification information, contact
National Credentialing Agency for Laboratory Personnel
PO Box 15945-289
Lenexa, KS 66285
Tel: 913-438-5110 ext. 647
Email: nca-info@goamp.com
http://www.nca-info.org

Nuclear Medicine Technologists

OVERVIEW

Nuclear medicine technologists prepare and administer chemicals known as radiopharmaceuticals (radioactive drugs) used in the diagnosis and treatment of certain diseases. These drugs are administered to a patient and are absorbed in specific locations in the patient's body, thus allowing technologists to use diagnostic equipment to image and analyze their concentration in certain tissues or organs. Technicians also perform laboratory tests on patients' blood and urine to determine certain body chemical levels. There are approximately 18,000 nuclear medicine technologists employed in the United States.

HISTORY

The origins of nuclear medicine can be traced to the turn of the 20th century when Marie Curie and her fellow scientists discovered radium. Radium, however, had no medical application until after World War II, when scientists discovered ways of producing artificial radionuclides. This led to the development of nuclear medicine.

In nuclear medicine, an image is transmitted that enables the physician to diagnose diseased tissue and functional disorders. Unlike X rays, however, where the radiation passes through the body to expose photographic film, in nuclear medicine the radiation comes from radioactive isotopes inside the body. A compound is made radioactive (called a radiopharmaceutical) and then is injected into or swallowed by the patient. The rates

QUICK FACTS

School Subjects
Biology
Computer science
Mathematics

Personal Skills
Helping/teaching
Technical/scientific

Work Environment
Primarily indoors
Primarily one location

Minimum Education Level
Associate's degree

Salary Range
$31,910 to $44,130 to $58,500+

Certification or Licensing
Required by certain states

Outlook
Faster than the average

DOT
078

GOE
10.02.02

NOC
3215

O*NET-SOC
29-2033.00

of absorption and elimination can be determined by measuring the radiation over a period of time with special cameras. This information is then used in the diagnosis and treatment of certain diseases, such as a dysfunctional thyroid gland or cancer.

All forms of radiation are potentially harmful, but carefully controlled and precisely directed doses of radiation are used with great

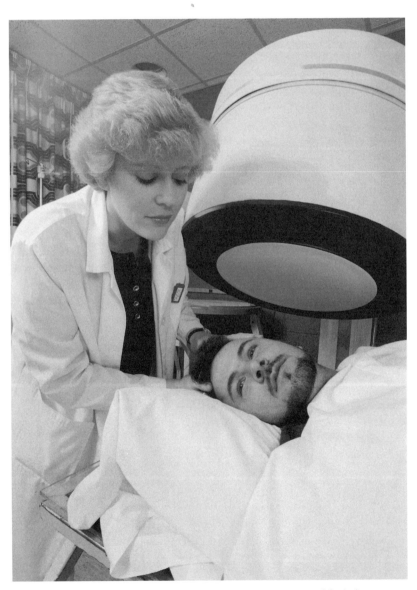

A nuclear medicine technologist administers treatment. (*Corbis*)

success. Professional technologists are educated in the use of nuclear medicine, which has dramatically changed health care.

THE JOB

Nuclear medicine technologists work directly with patients, preparing and administering radioactive drugs. A physician supervises all work. Because of the nature of radioactive material, the drug preparation requires adherence to strict safety precautions. All safety procedures are overseen by the Nuclear Regulatory Commission.

After administering the drug to the patient, the technologist operates a gamma scintillation camera that takes pictures of the radioactive drug as it passes through or accumulates in parts of the patient's body. These images are then displayed on a computer screen, where the technologist and physician can examine them. The images can be used to diagnose diseases or disorders in such organs as the heart, brain, lungs, liver, kidneys, and bones. Nuclear medicine is also used for therapeutic purposes, such as to destroy abnormal thyroid tissue or ease the pain of a terminally ill patient.

Nuclear medicine technologists also have administrative duties. They must document the procedures performed, check all diagnostic equipment and record its use and maintenance, and keep track of the radioactive drugs administered. These technologists may also perform laboratory testing of a patient's body specimens, such as blood or urine. In addition, they provide the attending physician with up-to-date medical records for his or her review.

REQUIREMENTS

High School

To prepare for this work, you should take plenty of high school classes in math and science, including algebra, geometry, biology, chemistry, and physics. If your school offers anatomy classes, take those as well. Health courses may also be beneficial. Because using technology will be a large part of this work, be sure to take computer science classes. Also, because you will have considerable interaction with patients as well as other health care professionals, take English courses to improve your communication skills.

Postsecondary Training

There are several ways to become a nuclear medicine technologist. You can complete at minimum a two-year certificate program, a two-year associate's degree program, or a four-year bachelor's degree program in nuclear medicine technology. Professional training is available at some colleges as part of a bachelor's or associate's program, and it ranges from two to four years in length. Some hospitals and technical schools also offer certificate training programs. Whatever program you decide to attend, make sure it is accredited by the Joint Review Committee on Educational Programs in Nuclear Medicine Technology (JRCNMT). Information on accredited programs is available at the JRCNMT website, http://www.jrcnmt.org.

Some educational programs are designed for individuals who already have a background in a related health care field, such as radiologic technology, sonography, or nursing. These programs are usually one year in length. A good knowledge of anatomy and physiology is helpful. Course work in nuclear medicine technologist programs includes radiation biology and protection, radioactivity and instrumentation, radiopharmaceuticals and their use on patients, and therapeutic nuclear medicine.

Certification or Licensing

Nuclear medicine technologists must know the minimum federal standards for use and administration of nuclear drugs and equipment. Twenty-one states now require technologists to be licensed. Certification or registration are also available through the Nuclear Medicine Technology Certification Board (NMTCB) and the American Registry of Radiologic Technologists (ARRT). Many nuclear medicine technologist positions, especially those in hospitals, are open only to certified or registered technologists. Information on becoming registered or certified is available from the ARRT and the NMTCB. (See the end of this article for contact information.)

Other Requirements

Those interested in a nuclear medicine technology career should have a strong sense of teamwork, compassion for others, and self-motivation.

EXPLORING

Individuals cannot get hands-on experience in this field without the necessary qualifications. However, it is possible to become familiar with the job responsibilities by talking with practicing nuclear medicine technologists or teachers involved in the field. In addition, volunteer experience at local hospitals or nursing homes provides a good introduction to what it is like to work in a health care setting.

EMPLOYERS

There are approximately 18,000 nuclear medicine technologists in the United States, with most employed by hospitals. Nuclear medicine technologists are employed at health clinics, nuclear medical equipment development facilities, research facilities, and private laboratories.

STARTING OUT

Graduates of specialized training programs and two- and four-year programs usually receive placement assistance from their educational institutions, which have a vested interest in placing as many graduates as possible. Help wanted ads in local papers and professional journals are also good sources of job leads, as is participation in professional organizations, which gives members opportunities to network.

ADVANCEMENT

Growth in the field of nuclear medicine should lead to advancement opportunities. Advancement usually takes the form of promotion to a supervisory position, with a corresponding increase in pay and responsibilities. Due to increased competition for positions in large metropolitan hospitals, technologists who work at these institutions may need to transfer to another hospital or city to secure a promotion. Hospitals in rural areas have much less competition for positions and therefore are more likely to give promotions.

Promotions, which are more easily attained by earning a bachelor's degree, are normally to positions of supervisor, chief technologist, or nuclear medicine department administrator. Some technologists may advance by leaving clinical practice to teach or work with equipment development and sales.

EARNINGS

Naturally, individual earnings vary based on factors such as a person's level of education and experience. Also, those who work overtime and on-call can add to their yearly income. The U.S. Department of Labor reports that the median annual salary for all nuclear medicine technologists was $44,130 in 2000. The lowest paid 10 percent of technologists earned less than $31,910 annually, and the highest paid 10 percent made more than $58,500 per year. The department also notes that the middle 50 percent of nuclear medicine technologists earned between $38,150 and

$52,190 annually. Typical benefits for hospital workers include health insurance, paid vacations and sick leave, and pension plans.

WORK ENVIRONMENT

Nuclear medicine technologists usually set their own schedules and can expect to work 35–40 hours a week, although larger hospitals often require overtime. Night and weekend work can also be expected. Because the job usually takes place inside a hospital or other health care facility, the environment is always clean and well lighted. The placing or positioning of patients on the diagnostic equipment is sometimes required, so a basic physical fitness level is necessary. There is a small chance of low-level contamination from the radioactive material or from the handling of body fluids. Strict safety precautions, including the use of shielded syringes and gloves and the wearing of badges that measure radiation, greatly reduce the risk of contamination.

OUTLOOK

According to the U.S. Department of Labor, employment of nuclear medicine technologists should grow faster than the average through 2010. The Society of Nuclear Medicine estimates that 10–12 million nuclear imaging and therapeutic procedures are performed in the United States each year. Advances in medical diagnostic procedures could lead to increased use of nuclear medicine technology in the diagnosis and treatment of more diseases, including cancer treatment and cardiology. In addition, as the country's population ages there will be a growing number of middle-aged and older persons, who are the main subjects of diagnostic tests. Thus there will be an increased demand for professionals to administer the procedures. Most new job opportunities are expected to be in areas with large hospitals.

FOR MORE INFORMATION

For information about career opportunities as a nuclear medicine technologist, contact
American Society of Radiologic Technologists
15000 Central Avenue, SE
Albuquerque, NM 87123-3917
Tel: 800-444-2778
Email: asrtbod@asrt.org
http://www.asrt.org

For information on certification and state licensing, contact the following organizations
American Registry of Radiologic Technologists
1255 Northland Drive
St. Paul, MN 55120-1155
Tel: 651-687-0048
http://www.arrt.org

Joint Review Committee on Educational Programs in Nuclear
    Medicine Technology
#1 Second Avenue East, Suite C
Polson, MT 59860-2320
Tel: 406-883-0003
http://www.jrcnmt.org

Nuclear Medicine Technology Certification Board
2970 Clairmont Road, Suite 935
Atlanta, GA 30329
Tel: 404-315-1739
Email: board@nmtcb.org
http://www.nmtcb.org

For information on nuclear medicine, professional development, and education, contact
Society of Nuclear Medicine
1850 Samuel Morse Drive
Reston, VA 20190-5316
Tel: 703-708-9000
http://www.snm.org

Orthotic and Prosthetic Technicians

QUICK FACTS

School Subjects
Art
Biology
Technical/shop

Personal Skills
Helping/teaching
Mechanical/manipulative

Work Environment
Primarily indoors
Primarily one location

Minimum Education Level
Some postsecondary training

Salary Range
$18,075 to $30,160 to
$41,140

Certification or Licensing
Voluntary

Outlook
Faster than the average

DOT
712

GOE
05.05.11

NOC
3219

O*NET-SOC
29-2091.00

OVERVIEW

Orthotic technicians and *prosthetic technicians* make, fit, repair, and maintain orthotic and prosthetic devices according to specifications and under the guidance of orthotists and prosthetists. Orthotic devices, sometimes also referred to as orthopedic appliances, are braces used to support weak or ineffective joints or muscles or to correct physical defects, such as spinal deformities. Prosthetic devices are artificial limbs and plastic cosmetic devices. These devices are designed and fitted to the patient by prosthetists or orthotists. Orthotic and prosthetic technicians read the specifications prepared by orthotists and prosthetists to determine the materials and tools required to make the device. Part of their work involves making models of patients' torsos, limbs, or amputated areas. Most of the technicians' efforts, however, go into the actual building of the devices. Some technicians specialize in either orthotic devices or prosthetic devices, while others are trained and able to work with both types.

A technician whose work is closely related to that of the orthotic and prosthetic technician is the *arch-support technician*. Arch-support technicians make steel arch supports to fit a patient's foot according to prescriptions supplied by podiatrists, prosthetists, or orthotists.

HISTORY

Throughout history, different societies have sought ways to replace lost limbs artificially and to support or correct the function of weak body parts. The ancient Egyptians, Greeks, and Romans studied and knew a great deal about dislocations, muscular paralysis, and other musculoskeletal disorders. The famous Greek physician Galen introduced some of the terms still used in the design of orthotic devices and described therapies to accompany their use. The Egyptians began experimenting with splints around 5,000 years ago, and archaeologists have discovered evidence that even prehistoric people made use of crude braces and splints.

The modern origins of both orthotics and prosthetics are usually traced to the 16th century French surgeon Ambroise Paré. Some of the orthotic and prosthetic devices dating from that century include metal corsets, splints made out of leather and other materials for deformities of the hips and legs, special shoes, and solid metal hands.

During the 17th century, there was rapid progress in the field of orthotics in England. This was spurred, at least in part, by the Poor Relief Act of 1601, which created certain kinds of government responsibility for the disabled. The introduction of splints and braces to treat deformities arising from rickets dates from this time. It was also during this era that leather-covered wooden hands and single metal hooks were introduced to replace lost hands.

During more recent centuries, improvements in design and materials have generally come during or after major wars, especially World War I and World War II. Following World War II, for instance, prosthetic designers discovered new lightweight plastics for use in artificial arms and hands. The process of cineplasty, in which a part of the control mechanism inside a mechanical prosthesis is attached to the end of a patient's bicep muscle, allows for finer control over the moving parts of the prosthesis. All of these developments have made prosthetics more sophisticated, useful, and lifelike.

Similar dramatic developments have occurred in the field of orthotics during the past two centuries. During the 19th century, some of the most famous practitioners in this field, such as Hugh Owen Thomas, Sir Robert Jones, and James Knight, developed many of the appliances and treatments we use today. Development in this field led to greater specialization; orthopedic surgeons began writing prescriptions for the kinds of braces needed by their patients. Orthotists then designed and built them.

As noted earlier, growth in both fields was spurred in the 20th century by the two world wars, the Korean War, and the Vietnam War. An increase in sports-related injuries and accidents resulting from the use of automobiles have also been factors. Finally, the new developments have allowed more ailments to be successfully treated with orthotics and prosthetics and have further stimulated growth of the field. This has led to yet further specialization and to the need for specially trained technicians to assist orthotists and prosthetists in their duties.

THE JOB

The work of orthotic and prosthetic technicians is similar to that of the skilled craftsworker. They usually have very limited contact with patients, spending most of their time working on the orthotic and prosthetic devices. Their job begins with reading the diagrams and specifications drawn up by the orthotist or prosthetist to determine the type of device to be built and what materials and tools are needed.

Technicians often make models, or casts, of patients' features to use in building the devices. They rely on these models when making plastic cosmetic replacements, such as ears, noses, or hands, and also in fitting artificial limbs to the patient's residual limbs. To make these models, technicians use a wax or plastic impression of a patient's amputated area. They make a mold from the impression and pour plaster into the mold to make the cast. In order to make sure that it matches the patient's body part, technicians may have to carve, grind, or build up parts of the model.

In building orthotic devices, technicians bend, weld, and cut pieces of metal or plastic in order to shape them into the structural components of the device. To do this, they use hammers, anvils, welding equipment, and saws. They then drill and tap holes into the components for rivets and then rivet the pieces together.

To ensure a proper fit of the device when finished, they often shape the plastic or metal parts around the cast model of the patient's torso or limbs. When the basic structure of the device has been assembled, they cover and pad the structure, using layers of rubber, felt, plastic, and leather. To build the component parts of prosthetic devices, technicians cut, carve, and grind wood, plastic, metal, and fabric. They may use rotary saws, cutting machines, and hand cutting tools. They drill and tap holes for rivets and screws; glue, bolt, weld, sew, and rivet parts together; and cover the prosthesis with layers of padding.

When prosthetic technicians finish building the basic device, they fit it with an outer covering, using sewing machines, riveting guns, and hand tools. When necessary, they mix pigments to duplicate the skin coloring of the patients, and they apply the pigments to the outer coverings of the prosthesis.

Both orthotic and prosthetic technicians must test their devices for freedom of movement, alignment of parts, and functional stability. They must also repair and maintain orthotic and prosthetic devices as directed by the orthotist or prosthetist.

Like orthotic and prosthetic technicians, arch-support technicians work with plaster casts. These are supplied by podiatrists, orthotists, and prosthetists. Working from these models, technicians determine the shape and size of the support to be built. They select stainless steel sheets of the correct thickness and cut the sheets to the necessary size. They hammer the steel in prescribed contours to form the support and check the accuracy of the fit against the model. They also polish the support with abrasive polishing wheels, glue protective leather pieces to it, and rivet additional leather pieces to it for additional patient comfort.

REQUIREMENTS

High School

While in high school, you should take as many shop classes as possible. Courses in metal shop, wood shop, and machine shop should provide a good background for working with materials and tools used in this profession. Math classes, especially algebra and geometry, will teach you to work with measurements and numbers. You may also want to take art classes to develop your eye-hand coordination, sense of design and proportions, and knowledge of materials such as leather, metals, and plastics. Biology, health, or anatomy classes will give you an understanding of the structure of the human body, which will be needed in your future career. Computer science courses will also be helpful, as computer technologies are used in the designing of devices. Because technicians work closely with orthotists and prosthetists, they need excellent communication skills and the ability to follow directions precisely. Therefore, you should take English classes to hone your writing and speaking skills and develop your ability to interpret directions.

Postsecondary Training

Following high school, you have two options. You may enroll in a two-year program of supervised clinical experience and training. This method, which is the most common, is basically on-the-job training, in which the trainee works under the supervision of a certified orthotist, prosthetist, or orthotist-prosthetist. After the two years of training are successfully completed, the trainee achieves technician status.

The second method is to enroll in a one- or two-year program of formal instruction leading to a certificate or associate's degree in orthotics-prosthetics technology. The programs typically include classes in anatomy and physiology, properties of materials, prosthetic and orthotic techniques, and building devices, as well as supervised clinical experience. Currently there are only four technician programs offered in the United States that are accredited by the National Commission on Orthotic and Prosthetic Education (NCOPE). For a listing of these schools, visit the NCOPE website, http://www.ncope.org. Because of the scarcity of training programs, a much smaller number of technicians choose this method of training to enter the field.

Certification or Licensing

There are presently no licensing requirements for orthotic and prosthetic technicians. There is, however, a program for voluntary registration conducted by the American Board for Certification in Orthotics and Prosthetics (commonly called ABC). Candidates must have a minimum of a high school diploma and must have completed either the two-year supervised on-the-job training program or a one- or two-year program of formal instruction in an NCOPE-accredited institution. In addition, all candidates must pass an examination administered by ABC. Depending on their area of concentration, technicians who pass the examination are designated as registered technician, orthotic (RTO), registered technician, prosthetic (RTP), or registered technician, prosthetic-orthotic (RTPO). To maintain registration, a technician must complete a certain number of ABC-approved professional continuing education credits every five years.

Other Requirements

To be a successful orthotic or prosthetic technician, you will need to enjoy working with your hands and have excellent eye-hand coordination. You must also be patient and detail oriented, since this work will involve using precise measurements and working on a piece until it is an exact fit. Technicians should be committed to lifelong learning, as new technologies, materials, and processes are continuously being developed. A good sense of color will also be helpful because your responsibilities may include matching the color of a device to a patient's skin tone.

EXPLORING

There are very few opportunities for people without training to get part-time or summer work in the orthotics and prosthetics field. Your first exposure to the work will probably be as part of a supervised training program or a clinical experience in a formal degree program. There are, however, some ways you can find out more about this kind of work. Teachers or guidance counselors can arrange a visit to a rehabilitation center or hospital with an orthotics and prosthetics department. On such a visit, you can see technicians at work and perhaps talk with them about what their jobs are like. You can also become familiar with the field by reading about it. For example, you might want to read an issue of or even subscribe to the *O&P Almanac* (http://www.aopanet.org/opalmanac/), a magazine published by the American Orthotic and Prosthetic Association that covers business, government, and professional news concerning the industry.

A very good way to gain some exposure to the health care field is to do volunteer work. Volunteer at your local hospital or a rehabilitation center where you will have the opportunity to interact with patients and staff. Even if your duties do not allow you to see patients at various stages of being fitted for a device, you will still benefit from the experience of working in a health care setting. Volunteering will also demonstrate your sincere interest in the field to training program admissions officers and future employers.

EMPLOYERS

Typical employers of prosthetic and orthotic technicians include hospitals, rehabilitation centers, private brace and limb companies, and the Veterans Health Administration.

STARTING OUT

Graduates of one- or two-year programs of formal instruction usually have the easiest time finding a first job. Teachers and placement offices will have valuable advice and information about local employers that they can share with students about to graduate. Also, check into some of the trade publications for the orthotics and prosthetics industry. These publications often carry classified advertising with listings of job openings.

If you have no prior experience and want to enter a supervised training program, you should contact hospitals, private brace and limb companies, and rehabilitation centers to inquire about programs. You might also watch the local newspapers for entry-level job openings in the field.

ADVANCEMENT

In some large orthotics and prosthetics departments in hospitals or rehabilitation centers, it is common to advance to the position of orthotic or prosthetic assistant after you have acquired enough experience. Another form of advancement might be specialization in a certain aspect of the work. In some cases, the experienced and skilled technician might be able to move into a supervisory position.

In general, however, significant advancement is open only to those who pursue additional training and education. With additional education and by meeting prescribed training requirements, technicians can become certified orthotists, certified prosthetists, or certified prosthetist-orthotists. Becoming an orthotist or prosthetist requires a four-year degree in orthotics or prosthetics or completion of a certificate course ranging in length from six months to one year.

Technicians working for the Veterans Health Administration or other state or federal agencies will find that advancement is conducted according to civil service rules and procedures.

EARNINGS

The salary level for orthotic and prosthetic technicians varies widely, depending on several factors. The most significant factor influencing salary level is certification. Technicians who have received their certification earn an average of approximately $3.50 more per hour than those who are noncertified, which translates into a difference of more than $7,000 yearly. Other factors influencing salary differences include area of the country where a technician works, size of employer, type of employer, and years of work experience. According to the *2000 O&P Business and Salary Survey Report* conducted by the American Orthotic and Prosthetic Association, certified technicians who had up to two years of work experience earned an average of $14.50 per hour. This hourly wage would translate into a yearly salary of approximately $30,160 for full-time work. Certified technicians with two to five years' experience earned an average of $17.61 per hour (approximately $36,630 annually). Those with more than five years of experience made an average of $19.78 an hour (approximately $41,140 per year). By comparison, the report also noted the lowest hourly pay for noncertified technicians with less than two years' experience averaged $8.69 per hour (approximately $18,075 annually).

Technicians working for the Veterans Health Administration or other federal agencies will find that their salaries are determined by their Government Service rating. Government Service ratings are determined by a number of factors including level of training, area of expertise, and performance on standardized tests.

WORK ENVIRONMENT

Orthotic and prosthetic technicians usually work five-day, 40-hour weeks. There typically is little need for overtime, weekend, or evening work.

Orthotic and prosthetic technicians spend much of their time in a workshop setting, which may be cluttered, loud, and dusty from the machinery and the cast-making. In some cases, they may have to work in uncomfortably hot oven rooms to soften the materials they use. They also work with power tools and sharp hand tools, which means that there is a chance of injury. However, careful adherence to safety procedures greatly reduces that risk.

Technicians usually work on their projects individually, but they do collaborate with the orthotist or prosthetist to make sure the finished product meets specifications. The actual contact with patients is handled by the orthotist or prosthetist, which may be a relief to some technicians. However, for some, this distance from the people they are trying to help may be a source of frustration.

The satisfactions of this job are in many ways similar to that of other skilled craftsworkers—the sense of pride that comes from a job well done. In addition, orthotic and prosthetic technicians have the satisfaction of knowing that their work is a direct source of help to people in need.

OUTLOOK

Employment for orthotic and prosthetic technicians is expected to grow at a rate faster than the average. The need for technicians is driven by such circumstances as the rapid growth of the health care industry, increasing access to medical and rehabilitation care through private and public insurance programs, improving technologies, and our country's aging population. According to a study prepared for National Commission on Prosthetic Education, by the year 2015, the aging Baby Boomer population will largely increase the demand for both orthotists and prosthetists. By 2020, the number of people who have an amputation and are in need of prostheses will increase by 47 percent.

In addition, continuing developments in this field will mean that more people with different kinds of disabilities will be candidates for new or improved orthotic and prosthetic devices. As the need for orthotic and prosthetic devices and the variety of the devices themselves grow, so will the demand for skilled technicians.

FOR MORE INFORMATION

For information on becoming a certified orthotic or prosthetic technician, contact
American Board for Certification in Orthotics and Prosthetics
330 John Carlyle Street, Suite 210
Alexandria, VA 22314
Tel: 703-836-7114
Email: info@abcop.org
http://www.abcop.org

For information on the monthly magazine O&P Almanac *and news relating to the field, contact*
American Orthotic and Prosthetic Association
330 John Carlyle Street, Suite 200
Alexandria, VA 22314
Tel: 571-431-0876
Email: info@aopanet.org
http://www.aopanet.org

For information on accredited programs and to read the newsletter, Noteworthy, *covering topics in the field, visit the following website:*
National Commission on Orthotic and Prosthetic Education
330 John Carlyle Street, Suite 200
Alexandria, VA 22314
Tel: 703-836-7114
http://www.ncope.org

INTERVIEW

Edward Haddon has been part of the orthotics profession for 33 years, working both as an orthtotics educator and in orthotics facilities in Minnesota and North Dakota. He is currently director of orthotic and prosthetic education at Century College in White Bear Lake, Minnesota. Mr. Haddon spoke with the editors of Careers in Focus: Medical Technicians *about his career.*

Q. How did you first become interested in this field?

A. My interest in the profession was sparked at the University of Minnesota. The university had just started a new collaborative bachelor's degree program that involved business, industry, and health professions. A student could receive credit towards a bachelor's degree by designing a structured course of independent study in a profession of their choice. The dean of the department told me that the Otto Bock and Winkley orthotic and prosthetic facilities were interested in providing a course of independent study in orthotics and prosthetics. I went and visited the facility and knew that orthotics was what I was destined to do. That was the start of not only my wonderful career path but also the beginning of what is now the department of orthotic and prosthetic education here at Century College.

Q. What are an orthotic technician's main job responsibilities?

A. The main job responsibility for an orthotic technician is to fabricate orthoses according to a physician prescription to ensure proper fit, maximum function, cosmesis, and workmanship. The orthotic technician is also responsible for the repair and maintenance of an orthosis. Technicians may also be responsible for maintaining a safe work environment by repairing and maintaining tools, equipment, and machinery in the fabrication laboratory. Many technicians are also in charge of ordering and stocking components and materials used in fabrication.

Q. In what kind of environment do orthotic technicians work?

A. Technicians work in a laboratory setting, which includes individual work stations as well as standard and specialty equipment, tools, and machinery. The size and complexity of these laboratories vary depending on the fabricating needs of the individual facilities. These facilities can be either privately owned, part of a larger multilocation business, or hospital based.

Q. What were your expectations entering this field? Are they much different from the realities?

A. My expectations were to use my interest in medicine along with my interest in working with my hands in a creative manor to help people with their physical challenges, to become an American Board for Certification certified orthotist, to learn orthotic techniques from as many sources as possible, and to share my knowledge with others.

Although my career path was not always what I anticipated, all my expectations have been realized. Being in education I am able to share my knowledge with others. Continuing orthotic and prosthetic education for this profession has been excellent. Our national organizations have provided a wide variety of life-long educational experiences for all orthotic and prosthetic professionals. I am a certified orthotist and I am able to use my talents in more creative ways than I ever imagined to help people. Looking back on my career, I can honestly say I would not change a thing.

Q. **What kind of education and training do students receive in your program?**

A. The education for orthotic technicians at Century College includes didactic and laboratory coursework combined with individualized instruction in the areas of lower limb, upper limb, and spinal orthotic fabrication. Each of these areas also contains instruction in anatomy, terminology, measurement forms, fabrication process, system alignment, suspension techniques, components, materials, repair and maintenance procedures.

The practicum section enables the student to practice the fabrication skills learned in the program in an actual work setting at an orthotic facility for a minimum of 160 hours.

Q. **What is the best way to find a job in this field? Are job prospects good?**

A. The outlook for employment is excellent. There are more positions for orthotic and prosthetic technicians than can be filled by all the graduates from all the orthotic and prosthetic technician programs. Many facilities will list their employment opportunities with accredited educational orthotic and prosthetic programs. Openings for technician positions are also listed in professional trade magazines and local newspapers.

Q. **What would you say are the most important skills and personal qualities for an orthotic or prosthetic technician?**

A. A technician must have good eye-hand coordination, an ability to think and work in three dimensions, and good problem-solving abilities.

Personal qualities should include an interest in working with your hands, making a positive difference in people's lives, being a self-starter, as well as being able to work as a member of a team of professionals.

Q. What are the pros and cons of this career?

A. On the plus side this is a very stable profession in terms of employment. There are more job opportunities than there are trained technicians to fill them. There are also an ever-increasing number of people who need orthotic and prosthetic treatment, which will increase job opportunities. The variety of the fabrications keeps interest in the job at a high level. There has always been a steady stream of new and exciting materials, products, and developments in the profession that enhance our fabrication abilities and help patients.

There are so few negatives it is hard to think of any that make a significant difference. One of the challenges in our profession is the unstable funding or payment of fees for orthotic and prosthetic services by government agencies and private insurance companies.

Q. What advice would you give to someone who is interested in pursuing this career?

A. First I would visit an orthotic and prosthetic facility in your area. Most facilities are happy to show you what the profession entails. Talk with orthotics patients, if you are able, to get their perspective on the profession. If you decide that this is for you, I would visit the National Commission on Orthotics and Prosthetic Education website at http://www.ncope.org/ to find an accredited orthotic and prosthetic educational institution that meets your needs. All will be glad to counsel you on your educational goals and provide information on their programs.

Phlebotomy Technicians

QUICK FACTS

School Subjects
Biology
Chemistry

Personal Skills
Helping/teaching
Technical/scientific

Work Environment
Primarily indoors
Primarily one location

Minimum Education Level
Some postsecondary training

Salary Range
$16,848 to $20,592 to
$40,000+

Certification or Licensing
Required by certain states

Outlook
About as fast as the average

DOT
079

GOE
02.04.02

NOC
3212

O*NET-SOC
N/A

OVERVIEW

Phlebotomy technicians, sometimes called phlebotomists, draw blood from patients or donors in hospitals, blood banks, clinics, physicians' offices, or other facilities. They assemble equipment, verify patient identification numbers, and withdraw blood either by puncturing a person's finger, or by extracting blood from a vein or artery with a needle syringe. They label, transport, and store blood for analysis or for other medical purposes.

HISTORY

Ancient people did not understand the role of blood, but they knew it was vital. Some believed that it might even be the home of the soul. Early Egyptians bathed in blood, hoping this act would cure illness or reverse the aging process. Some Romans drank the blood of dying gladiators in order to acquire the athletes' strength and bravery. Over time, scientists began to understand how blood functioned and they searched for ways to collect it or transfer it from one person to another. The methods they used, the lack of sterile procedures, and their limited knowledge sometimes resulted in the death of the donor as well as the patient.

Modern techniques of blood collection, typing, and transfusion developed only within this century. Today there are professionals called phlebotomy technicians who draw blood and work in clean, well-lighted laboratories, hospitals, and clinics.

THE JOB

The first step a phlebotomy technician performs when drawing blood is to take the patient's medical history, temperature, and pulse and match the physician's testing order with the amount of blood to be drawn. Next, the site of the withdrawal is located. Typically, the large vein that is visible on the underside of the arm near the elbow is used.

Finding a suitable vein, however, is not always easy because there are many anatomical differences among people. Once a suitable site is located, a tourniquet is wrapped high on the patient's upper arm. The phlebotomy technician checks the site for lesions, scar tissue, other needle marks, and any skin disorders that might interfere with the collection process. Then the site is cleansed by swabbing with a sterile solution. The technician positions the patient's arm in order to make a proper puncture. The needle is inserted almost parallel to the vein and as close to the skin as possible. Then the hub of the needle is raised and the angle toward the skin increased so that the needle can pierce the wall of the vein. After the needle is advanced slightly into the vein, blood may be withdrawn. Generally this is done by releasing a clamp attached to the blood collection device or to the tubing. When the required amount of blood is collected, the needle is removed and sealed, the site covered, and the tourniquet removed.

After collection, the phlebotomy technician labels the blood, coordinates its number with the worksheet order, and transports the blood to a storage facility or to another laboratory worker. The phlebotomy technician also checks to make sure that the patient is all right, notes any adverse reactions, and administers first aid or other medical assistance when necessary.

REQUIREMENTS

High School

Biology, health, and other science courses are helpful if you wish to become a phlebotomy technician after graduation. Computer science, English, and speech classes are also important. In addition, if you plan on entering formal phlebotomy training programs, you should take the courses that fulfill the entrance requirements for the program you plan to attend.

Postsecondary Training

Until recently, on-the-job training was the norm for phlebotomy technicians. Now, formal programs are offered through independent training schools, community colleges, or hospitals. Most programs last from 10 weeks to one year. They include both in-class study and supervised, clinical practice. Course work includes anatomy, physiology, introduction to laboratory practices, communication, medical terminology, phlebotomy techniques, emergency situations, and CPR training.

Certification or Licensing

Certification and licensing for phlebotomy technicians varies according to state and employer. Several agencies grant certification, including American Medical Technologists, the American Society of Phlebotomy Technicians, and the Board of Registry of the American Society of Clinical Pathology. Contact the organizations for more information.

Other Requirements

To be a successful phlebotomy technician, you should enjoy working with people and be an effective communicator and a good listener. You should also be attentive to detail and be able to work under pressure. In addition, you should have patience and good manual dexterity.

EXPLORING

Volunteer at a hospital or other health care setting to get experience in and exposure to patient care techniques, medical procedures, and safety precautions. Take first aid and CPR classes.

Visit the American Association of Blood Banks website listed at the end of this article to learn facts about blood and blood donation. Become a frequent blood donor and use the opportunity to talk to the phlebetomist who draws your blood about his or her job.

EMPLOYERS

Phlebotomy technicians work in a variety of health care settings. The majority of them work in hospitals or in outpatient settings such as clinics, physicians' offices, reference laboratories, or blood banks. A few are hired by private industry or by insurance companies. The greatest need for phlebotomy technicians is in small hospitals (fewer than 100 beds).

STARTING OUT

Many of the publications serving health care professionals list job advertisements, as do daily newspapers. In addition, some employers actively recruit employees by contacting students who are graduating from accredited programs. Some programs offer job-placement assistance, as well.

ADVANCEMENT

At some hospitals, phlebotomy technicians advance through several different levels of responsibility and pay, depending on their training and experience.

One of the most common career paths for phlebotomy technicians is to work for a few years in a hospital or laboratory and then return to school to study medical laboratory technology or some other branch of clinical laboratory medicine.

There may also be supervisory advancement opportunities within blood bank centers. For example, you can return to school, obtain a bachelor's degree, attend a specialized fifth-year program, and become a certified specialist in blood bank technology.

EARNINGS

Experience, level of education, employer, and work performed determine the salary ranges for phlebotomy technicians. According to a survey by the American Society of Clinical Pathology's Board of Registry, the median beginning hourly salary for phlebotomy technicians was $8.10 in 2000. The median hourly salary for more experienced workers was $9.90. The highest paid phlebotomy technicians earned $11.80 or more per hour. Pay rates vary depending on geographic location.

A specialist in blood bank technology with a bachelor's degree and advanced training can usually expect a starting salary of approximately $40,000 a year.

Benefits such as vacation time, sick leave, insurance, and other fringe benefits vary by employer, but are usually consistent with other full-time health care workers.

WORK ENVIRONMENT

Most phlebotomy technicians are supervised by other laboratory personnel and work in hospitals, clinics, doctors' offices, reference laboratories, and blood banks. Some technicians may be required to work shifts. If they work for a blood bank, they may be required to travel to other sites for a blood drive.

OUTLOOK

The demand for phlebotomy technicians in the United States is highest in small hospitals. As the percentage of our population aged 65 or older continues to rise, the demand for all kinds of health care professionals will increase as well. There is a demand for workers who are qualified to draw blood at the bedside of patients. The growing number of patients with certain diseases, such as HIV and AIDS, also increases the need for phlebotomy technicians.

FOR MORE INFORMATION

The following organizations provide information on phlebotomy technician careers, certification, and employment opportunities.

American Association of Blood Banks
8101 Glenbrook Road
Bethesda, MD 20814-2749
Tel: 301-907-6977
Email: aabb@aabb.org
http://www.aabb.org

American Medical Technologists
710 Higgins Road
Park Ridge, IL 60068-5765
Tel: 847-823-5169
Email: mail@amt1.com
http://www.amt1.com

American Society for Clinical Laboratory Science
6701 Democracy Boulevard, Suite 300
Bethesda, MD 20817
Tel: 301-657-2768
Email: ascls@ascls.org
http://www.ascls.org

American Society of Phlebotomy Technicians
PO Box 1831
Hickory, NC 28603
Tel: 828-294-0078
http://www.aspt.org

For information on accredited training programs, contact
National Accrediting Agency for Clinical Laboratory Sciences
8410 West Bryn Mawr Avenue, Suite 670
Chicago, IL 60631
Tel: 773-714-8880
Email: info@naacls.org
http://www.naacls.org

Psychiatric Technicians

QUICK FACTS

School Subjects
Health
Psychology

Personal Skills
Communication/ideas
Helping/teaching

Work Environment
Primarily indoors
Primarily one location

Minimum Education Level
Some postsecondary training

Salary Range
$16,150 to $24,420 to
$39,310+

Certification or Licensing
Required by certain states

Outlook
More slowly than the average

DOT
079

GOE
10.02.02

NOC
3413

O*NET-SOC
29-2053.00, 31-1013.00

OVERVIEW

Psychiatric technicians work with mentally ill, emotionally disturbed, or developmentally disabled people. Their duties vary considerably depending on place of work but may include helping patients with hygiene and housekeeping and recording a patients' pulses, temperatures, and respiration rates. Psychiatric technicians participate in treatment programs by having one-on-one sessions with patients, under a nurse's or counselor's direction.

Another prime aspect of the psychiatric technician's work is reporting observations of patients' behavior to medical and psychiatric staff. Psychiatric technicians may also fill out admitting forms for new patients, contact patients' families to arrange conferences, issue medications from the dispensary, and maintain records. There are approximately 54,000 psychiatric technicians employed in the United States.

HISTORY

Although some mentally ill people were treated as early as the 15th century in institutions like the Hospital of Saint Mary of Bethlehem in London (whose name was often shortened to Bedlam), the practice of institutionalizing people with mental disorders did not become common until the 17th century. During the 17th, 18th, and even into the 19th centuries, treatment of mentally ill patients was quite crude and often simply barbarous. This state of affairs started to change as medical practitioners began to see mental illness as a medical problem. During the late 18th and early 19th centuries, hospitals began concentrating on keeping patients clean and comfortable, building their self-respect, and treating them with friendliness and encouragement. This method of treating mental illness resulted in the establishment of specially designed institutions for the care of mental patients.

Beginning in the 1940s, mental health institutions sought more effective therapeutic services for their patients, including more social activities and innovative treatment programs. Treatment shifted from a sole reliance on state mental hospitals to provision of more services in general hospitals and community mental health centers.

The object was to shorten periods of institutionalization and to decrease the stigma and dislocation associated with treatment in mental hospitals. However, these changes also sharply increased personnel needs. One strategy for dealing with this has been to train more professionals: psychiatrists, psychologists, social workers, nurses, and others. Another strategy has focused on training more nonprofessionals: aides, attendants, orderlies, and others.

The drive to develop new therapies and the trend toward deinstitutionalizing patients have led to the creation of a new category of mental health worker with a training level between that of the professional and the nonprofessional. Workers at this level are usually referred to as paraprofessionals or technicians, and in the mental health field they are known as psychiatric technicians or mental health technicians.

THE JOB

Psychiatric technicians not only take over for or assist professionals in traditional treatment activities but also provide new services in innovative ways.

They may work with alcohol and drug abusers, psychotic or emotionally disturbed children and adults, developmentally disabled people, or the aged. They must be skilled and specially trained.

Psychiatric technicians are supervised by health professionals, such as registered nurses, counselors, therapists, or, more and more frequently, senior psychiatric technicians. Psychiatric technicians work as part of a team of mental health care workers and provide physical and mental rehabilitation for patients through recreational, occupational, and psychological readjustment programs.

In general, psychiatric technicians help plan and implement individual treatment programs. Specific activities vary according to work setting, but they may include the following: interviewing and information gathering; working in a hospital unit admitting, screening, evaluating, or discharging patients; record keeping; making referrals to community agencies; working for patients' needs and rights; visiting patients at home after their release from a hospital; and participating in individual and group counseling and therapy.

Psychiatric technicians endeavor to work with patients in a broad, comprehensive manner and to see each patient as a person whose peculiar or abnormal behavior stems from an illness or disability. They strive to help each patient achieve a maximum level of functioning. This means helping patients strengthen social and mental skills, accept greater responsibility, and develop confidence to enter into social, educational, or vocational activities.

In addition, psychiatric technicians working in hospitals handle a certain number of nursing responsibilities. They may take temperature, pulse and respiration rates; measure blood pressure; and help administer medications and physical treatments. In many cases, technicians working in hospitals will find themselves concerned with all aspects of their patients' lives—from eating, sleeping, and personal hygiene to developing social skills and improving self-image.

Technicians working in clinics, community mental health centers, halfway houses, day hospitals, or other noninstitutional settings also perform some activities special to their situation. They interview newly registered patients and patient relatives and visit patients and their families at home. They also administer psychological tests, participate in group activities, and write reports about their observations to supervising psychiatrists or other mental health professionals. They try to ease the transition of patients leaving hospitals and returning to their communities. They may refer patients to and arrange for consultations with mental health specialists. They may also help patients resolve problems with employment, housing, and personal finance.

Most psychiatric technicians are trained as generalists in providing mental health services. But some opportunities exist for technicians to specialize in a particular aspect of mental health care. For example, some psychiatric technicians specialize in the problems of mentally disturbed children. Others work as counselors in drug and alcohol abuse programs or as members of psychiatric emergency or crisis-intervention teams.

Another area of emphasis is working in community mental health. Technicians employed in this area are sometimes known as *human services technicians*. They use rehabilitation techniques for nonhospitalized patients who have problems adjusting to their social environment. These technicians may be primarily concerned with drug and alcohol abuse, parental effectiveness, the elderly, or problems in interpersonal relationships. Human services technicians work in social welfare departments, child care centers, preschools, vocational rehabilitation workshops, and schools for the learning disabled, emotionally disturbed, and mentally handicapped. This concentration is particularly popular in college curricula, according to the American Association of Psychiatric Technicians (AAPT), although it has yet to find wide acceptance in the job market.

With slightly different training, psychiatric technicians may specialize in the treatment of developmentally disabled people. These technicians, sometimes referred to as DD techs, work with patients by doing such things as teaching recreational activities. They generally work in halfway houses, state hospitals, training centers, or state and local service agencies. These jobs are among the easiest psychiatric technician jobs to get, and many techs start out in this area. On average, however, the pay of the DD tech is considerably less than that of other psychiatric technicians.

REQUIREMENTS

High School

A high school diploma is the minimum education requirement to find work as a psychiatric technician, although in many cases psychiatric technicians are expected to have two years of training beyond high school. In general, high school students should take courses in English, biology, psychology, and sociology.

Postsecondary Training

The two-year postsecondary training programs usually lead to an associate of arts or associate of science degree. It is important to note that many hospitals prefer to hire applicants with bachelor's degrees.

In general, study programs include human development, personality structure, the nature of mental illness, and, to a limited extent, anatomy, physiology, basic nursing, and medical science. Other subjects usually include some introduction to basic social sciences so that technicians can better understand relevant family and community structures, an overview of the structure and functions of institutions that treat patients, and most importantly, practical instruction.

Certification and Licensing

Psychiatric technicians must be licensed in California, Colorado, Kansas, and Arkansas. Ask your guidance or placement counselors for more information about licensing requirements in your state. Voluntary certification is available through the American Association of Psychiatric Technicians. To receive certification, you will need to take a written exam covering topics on mental disorders and developmental disabilities. Those who pass the test receive the designation nationally certified psychiatric technician and can place the initials NCPT after their names. Depending on the employer, a certified technician may qualify for higher pay than a noncertified worker.

Most mental health technology programs emphasize interviewing skills. Interview training enables technicians to observe and record accurately a patient's tone of voice and body language; this data will then be interpreted by the treatment team and sometimes even a court of law. Some programs also teach administration of selected psychological tests. You may also gain knowledge and training in crisis intervention techniques, child guidance, group counseling, family therapy, behavior modification, and consultation skills.

Other Requirements

Because psychiatric technicians interact with people, you must be sensitive to others' needs and feelings. Some aspects of sensitivity can be learned, but this requires a willingness to listen, being extremely observant, and risking involvement in situations that at first may seem ambiguous and confusing. In addition, you need to be willing to look at your own attitudes and behaviors and to be flexible and open about effecting changes in them. The more you know about yourself, the more effective you will be in helping others.

Patience, understanding, and a "thick skin" are required in working with people who may be disagreeable and unpleasant because of their illnesses. Patients can be particularly adept at finding a person's weaknesses and exploiting them. This is not a job for the tenderhearted. A sense of responsibility and the ability to remain calm in emergencies are also essential characteristics.

EXPLORING

Prospective psychiatric technicians can gather personal experience in this field in a number of ways. You can apply for a job as a nurse's aide at a local general hospital. In this way you gain direct experience providing patient care. If such a job requires too much of a time commitment, you might consider volunteering at a hospital part time or during the summer. Volunteering is an excellent way to become acquainted with the field, and many techs' full-time jobs evolve from volunteer positions. Most volunteers must be 21 years of age to work in the mental health unit. Younger students who are interested in volunteering can often find places in the medical records department or other areas to get their feet in the door.

People interested in this career might also consider volunteering at their local mental health association or a local social welfare agency. In some cases, the mental health association can arrange opportunities for volunteer work inside a mental hospital or mental health clinic. Finally, either on your own or with your teachers, you can arrange a visit to a mental health clinic. You may be able to talk with staff members and observe firsthand how psychiatric technicians do their jobs.

EMPLOYERS

Psychiatric technicians work in a variety of settings: the military, hospitals, mental hospitals, community mental health centers, psychiatric clinics, schools and day centers for the developmentally disabled, and social service agencies. They also work at residential and nonresidential centers, such as geriatric nursing homes, child or adolescent development centers, and halfway houses.

Other potential places of employment for psychiatric technicians include correctional programs and juvenile courts, schools for the blind and deaf, community action programs, family service centers, and public housing programs.

STARTING OUT

Graduates from mental health and human services technology programs can usually choose from a variety of job possibilities. College placement officers can be extremely helpful in locating employment. Students can follow want ads or apply directly to the clinics, agencies, or hospitals of their choice. Job information can also be obtained from the department of mental health in each state.

ADVANCEMENT

Working as a psychiatric technician is still a relatively new occupation, and sequences of promotions have not yet been clearly defined. Seeking national certification through the AAPT is one way to help to set up a career path in this field. Advancement normally takes the form of being given greater responsibilities with less supervision. It usually results from gaining experience, developing competence and leadership abilities, and continuing formal and practical education. In cases where promotions are governed by civil service regulations, advancement is based on experience and test scores on promotion examinations.

In large part, advancement is linked to gaining further education. Thus, after working a few years, technicians may decide to obtain a bachelor's degree in psychology. Advanced education, coupled with previous training and work experience, greatly enhance advancement potential. For instance, with a bachelor's degree, experienced technicians may be able to find rewarding positions as instructors in programs to train future mental health workers.

EARNINGS

Salaries for psychiatric technicians vary according to geographical area and work setting: technicians in California generally receive substantially higher wages than those in other areas of the country, and technicians in community settings generally receive higher salaries than those in institutional settings. The U.S. Department of Labor reports that psychiatric technicians earned median salaries of $24,420 in 2000. The lowest 10 percent earned less than $16,150, and the highest 10 percent earned $39,310 or more.

Most psychiatric technicians receive fringe benefits, including health insurance, sick leave, and paid vacations. Technicians working for state institutions or agencies will probably also be eligible for financial assistance for further education.

WORK ENVIRONMENT

Psychiatric technicians work in a variety of settings, and their working conditions vary accordingly. Typically they work 40 hours a week, five days a week, although one may be a weekend day. Some psychiatric technicians work evening or night shifts, and all technicians may sometimes be asked to work holidays.

For the most part, the physical surroundings are pleasant. Most institutions, clinics, mental health centers, and agency offices are kept clean and comfortably furnished. Technicians who work with the mentally ill must nonetheless adjust to an environment that is normally chaotic and sometimes upsetting. Some patients are acutely depressed and withdrawn or excessively agitated and excited. Some patients may become unexpectedly violent and verbally abusive. However, institutions treating these kinds of patients maintain enough staff to keep the patients safe and to protect workers from physical harm. Psychiatric technicians who make home visits also may sometimes confront unpleasant conditions.

Finally, psychiatric technicians work not only with individuals but often with the community. In that role, technicians can be called upon to advocate for their patients by motivating community agencies to provide services or by obtaining exceptions to rules when needed for individuals or groups of patients. Successful psychiatric technicians become competent in working and dealing with various decision-making processes of community and neighborhood groups.

OUTLOOK

The U.S. Department of Labor projects employment for psychiatric technicians to grow more slowly than the average through 2010. Demand for technicians, though, is expected to continue in large part because of a well-established trend of returning hospitalized patients to their communities after shorter and shorter periods of hospitalization. This trend has encouraged development of comprehensive community mental health centers and has led to a strong demand for psychiatric technicians to staff these facilities.

Concerns over rising health care costs should increase employment levels for technicians, because they and other paraprofessionals can take over some functions of higher paid professionals. This kind of substitution has been proven to be an effective way of reducing costs without reducing quality of care.

FOR MORE INFORMATION

For more information on the career, contact this organization:
California Association of Psychiatric Technicians
2000 "O" Street, Suite 250
Sacramento, CA 95814-5286
Tel: 916-329-9140
http://www.psych-health.com

Radiologic Technologists

QUICK FACTS

School Subjects
Biology
Mathematics

Personal Skills
Helping/teaching
Technical/scientific

Work Environment
Primarily indoors
Primarily one location

Minimum Education Level
Some postsecondary training

Salary Range
$25,310 to $36,000 to
$52,050+

Certification or Licensing
Voluntary (certification)
Required by certain states
(licensing)

Outlook
Faster than the average

DOT
078

GOE
02.04.01

NOC
3215

O*NET-SOC
29-2034.01

OVERVIEW

Radiologic technologists operate equipment that creates images of a patient's body tissues, organs, and bones for the purpose of medical diagnoses and therapies. These images allow physicians to know the exact nature of a patient's injury or disease, such as the location of a broken bone or the confirmation of an ulcer.

Before an X-ray examination, radiologic technologists may administer drugs or chemical mixtures to the patient to better highlight internal organs. They place the patient in the correct position between the X-ray source and film and protect body areas that are not to be exposed to radiation. After determining the proper duration and intensity of the exposure, they operate the controls to beam X rays through the patient and expose the photographic film.

They may operate computer-aided imaging equipment that does not involve X rays and may help to treat diseased or affected areas of the body by exposing the patient to specified concentrations of radiation for prescribed times. Radiologic technologists and technicians hold about 167,000 jobs in the United States.

HISTORY

Radiography uses a form of electromagnetic radiation to create an image on a photographic film. Unlike photography, where the film is exposed to ordinary light rays (the most familiar kind of electromagnetic radiation), in radiography the

148

film is exposed to X rays, which have shorter wavelengths and different energy levels.

X rays were discovered by Wilhelm Conrad Roentgen in 1895. X rays, or roentgen rays, are generated in a glass vacuum tube (an X-ray tube) that contains two differently charged electrodes, one of which gives off electrons. When the electrons travel from one electrode to the other, some of the energy they emit is x-radiation. X rays are able to pass through skin and muscle and other soft body tissue, while bones and denser objects show up as white images on the photographic emulsion when film is exposed to X rays. A picture of the inside of the body can thus be developed.

All forms of radiation are potentially harmful. Exposure to ultraviolet radiation may tan the skin, but it can also result in burning and other damage to tissue, including the development of cancer cells. Low-level infrared radiation can warm tissues, but at higher levels it cooks them like microwaves do; the process can destroy cells. Protective measures to avoid all unnecessary exposure to radiation must be taken whenever X rays are used, because they can have both short- and long-term harmful effects.

There are other forms of diagnostic imaging that do not expose patients to any potentially harmful radiation. Sound waves are used in ultrasound technology, or sonography, to obtain a picture of internal organs. High-frequency sound waves beamed into the patient's body bounce back and create echoes that can be recorded on a paper strip or photograph. Ultrasound is very frequently employed to determine the size and development of a human fetus. Magnetic resonance imaging (MRI) uses magnetic fields, radio waves, and computers to create images of the patient's body.

The use of imaging techniques that do not involve radiation grew rapidly during the 1980s and 1990s because of the safety of these techniques and because of great improvements in computer technology. Computers can now handle a vast quantity of data much more rapidly, making it possible to enhance images to great clarity and sharpness.

THE JOB

All radiological work is done at the request of and under the supervision of a physician. Just as a prescription is required for certain drugs to be dispensed or administered, so must a physician's request be issued before a patient can receive any kind of imaging procedure.

There are four primary disciplines in which radiologic technologists may work: radiography (taking X-ray pictures or radiographs), nuclear medicine, radiation therapy, and sonography. In each of these, the technologist works under the direction of a physician who specializes in interpreting the pictures produced by X rays, other imaging techniques, or radiation therapy. Technologists can work in more than one of these areas. Some technologists specialize in working with a particular part of the body or a specific condition.

X-ray pictures, or radiographs, are the most familiar use of radiologic technology. They are used to diagnose and determine treatment for a wide variety of afflictions, including ulcers, tumors, and bone fractures. Chest X-ray pictures can determine whether a person has a lung disease. Radiologic technologists who operate X-ray equipment first help the patient prepare for the radiologic examination. After explaining the procedure, they may administer a substance that makes the part of the body being imaged more clearly visible on the film. They make sure that the patient is not wearing jewelry or other metal that would obstruct the X-rays. They position the person sitting, standing, or lying down so that the correct view of the body can be radiographed, and then they cover adjacent areas with lead shielding to prevent unnecessary exposure to radiation.

The technologist positions the X-ray equipment at the proper angle and distance from the part to be radiographed and determines exposure time based on the location of the particular organ or bone and thickness of the body in that area. The controls of the X-ray machine are set to produce pictures of the correct density, contrast, and detail. Placing the photographic film closest to the body part being X-rayed, the technologist takes the requested images, repositioning the patient as needed. Typically, there are standards regarding the number of views to be taken of a given body part. The film is then developed for the radiologist or other physician to interpret.

In a fluoroscopic examination (a more complex imaging procedure that examines the gastrointestinal area), a beam of X-rays passes through the body and onto a fluorescent screen, enabling the physician to see the internal organs in motion. For these, the technologist first prepares a solution of barium sulfate to be administered to the patient, either rectally or orally, depending on the exam. The barium sulfate increases the contrast between the digestive tract and surrounding organs, making the image clearer. The technologist follows the physician's guidance in positioning the patient, monitors the machine's controls, and takes any follow-up radiographs as needed.

Radiologic technologists may learn other imaging procedures such as computed tomography (CT) scanning, which uses X-rays to get detailed cross-sectional images of the body's internal structures, and MRI, which uses radio waves, powerful magnets, and computers to obtain images of body parts. These diagnostic procedures are becoming more common and usually require radiologic technologists to undergo additional on-the-job training.

Other specialties within the radiography discipline include mammography and cardiovascular interventional technology. In addition, some technologists may focus on radiography of joints and bones, or they may be involved in such areas as angiocardiography (visualization of the heart and large blood vessels) or neuroradiology (the use of radiation to diagnose diseases of the nervous system).

Radiologic technologists perform a wide range of duties, from greeting patients and putting them at ease by explaining the procedures to developing the finished film. Their administrative tasks include maintaining patients' records, recording equipment usage and maintenance, organizing work schedules, and managing a radiologist's private practice or hospital's radiology department. Some radiologic technologists teach in programs to educate other technologists.

REQUIREMENTS

High School

If this career interests you, take plenty of math and science classes in high school. Biology, chemistry, and physics classes will be particularly useful to you. Take computer classes to become comfortable working with this technology. English classes will help you improve your communication skills. You will need these skills both when interacting with the patients and when working as part of a health care team. Finally, consider taking photography classes. Photography classes will give you experience with choosing film, framing an image, and the developing process.

Postsecondary Training

After high school, you will need to complete an education program in radiography. Programs range in length from two to four years. Depending on length, the programs award a certificate, associate's degree, or bachelor's degree. Two-year associate's degree programs are the most popular.

Educational programs are available in hospitals, medical centers, colleges and universities, and vocational and technical institutes. It is also possible to get radiologic technology training in the armed forces.

To enter an accredited program, you must be a high school graduate; some programs require one or two years of higher education. Courses in radiologic technology education programs include anatomy, physiology, patient care, physics, radiation protection, medical ethics, principles of imaging, medical terminology, radiobiology, and pathology. For some supervisory or administrative jobs in this field, a bachelor's or master's degree may be required.

Certification or Licensing

Radiologic technologists can become certified through the American Registry of Radiologic Technologists (ARRT) after graduating from an accredited program in radiography, radiation therapy, or nuclear medicine. After becoming certified, many technologists choose to register with the ARRT. Registration is an annual procedure required to maintain the certification. Registered technologists meet the following three criteria: they agree to comply with the ARRT rules and regulations, comply with the ARRT standards of ethics, and meet continuing education requirements. Only technologists who are currently registered can designate themselves as ARRT Registered Technologists and use the initials RT after their names. Although registration and certification are voluntary, many jobs are open only to technologists who have acquired these credentials.

In addition to being registered in the various imaging disciplines, radiologic technologists can receive advanced qualifications in each of the four radiography specializations: mammography, CT, MRI, and cardiovascular interventional technology. As the work of radiologic technologists grows increasingly complex and employment opportunities become more competitive, the desirability of registration and certification will also grow.

An increasing number of states have set up licensing requirements for radiologic technologists. According to the American Society of Radiologic Technologists, 35 states and Puerto Rico require radiologic technologists to be licensed. You will need to check with the state in which you hope to work about specific requirements there.

Other Requirements

Radiologic technologists should be responsible individuals with a mature and caring nature. They should be personable and enjoy interacting with all types of people, including those who are very ill. A compassionate attitude is essential to deal with patients who may be frightened or in pain.

EXPLORING

There is no way to gain direct experience in this profession without the appropriate qualifications. However, it is possible to learn about the duties of radiologic technologists by talking with them and observing the facilities and equipment they use. It is also possible to have interviews with teachers of radiologic technology. Ask your guidance counselor or a science teacher to help you contact local hospitals or

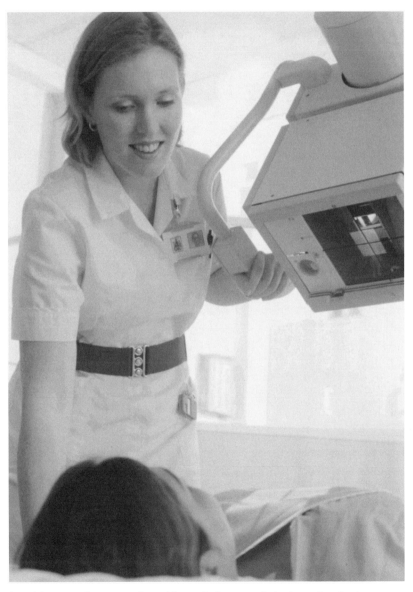

In addition to having technical knowledge, a radiologic technologist must be compassionate and adept at working with many types of personalities. (*Corbis*)

schools with radiography programs to locate technologists who are willing to talk to an interested student.

As with any career in health care, volunteering at a local hospital, clinic, or nursing home provides an excellent opportunity for you to explore your interest in the field. Most hospitals are eager for volunteers, and working in such a setting will give you a chance to see health care professionals in action as well as to have some patient contact.

EMPLOYERS

There are approximately 167,000 radiologic technologists working in the United States. According to the U.S. Department of Labor, more than half of these technologists work in hospitals. Radiologic technologists also find employment in doctors' offices and clinics, at X-ray labs, and in nursing homes.

STARTING OUT

With more states regulating the practice of radiologic technology, certification by the appropriate accreditation body for a given specialty is quickly becoming a necessity for employment. If you get your training from a school that lacks accreditation or if you learn on the job, you may have difficulty in qualifying for many positions, especially those with a wide range of assignments. If you are enrolled in a hospital educational program, you may be able to get a job with the hospital upon completion of the program. If you are in a degree program, you can get help finding a job through your school's placement office.

ADVANCEMENT

More than half of all radiologic technologists are employed in hospitals where there are opportunities for advancement to administrative and supervisory positions such as chief technologist or technical administrator. Other technologists develop special clinical skills in advanced imaging procedures, such as CT scanning or MRI. Some radiologic technologists qualify as instructors. Radiologic technologists who hold bachelor's degrees have more opportunities for advancement. The technologist who wishes to become a teacher or administrator will find that a master's degree and considerable experience are necessary.

EARNINGS

Salaries for radiologic technologists compare favorably with those of similar health care professionals. According to the U.S. Department of Labor, median annual earnings of radiologic technologists and technicians were $36,000 in 2000. The lowest paid 10 percent, which typically includes those just starting out in the field, earned less than $25,310. The highest paid 10 percent, which typically includes those with considerable experience, earned more than $52,050.

Median annual earnings of radiologic technologists and technicians who worked in medical and dental laboratories were $39,400 in 2000. Those who worked in hospitals earned a median of $36,280, and those who worked in offices and clinics of medical doctors earned $34,870.

Most technologists take part in their employers' vacation and sick leave provisions. In addition, most employers offer benefits such as health insurance and pensions.

WORK ENVIRONMENT

Full-time technologists generally work eight hours a day, 40 hours a week. In addition, they may be on call for some night emergency duty or weekend hours, which pays in equal time off or additional compensation.

In diagnostic radiologic work, technologists perform most of their tasks while on their feet. They move around a lot and often are called upon to lift patients who need help in moving.

Great care is exercised to protect technologists from radiation exposure. Each technologist wears a badge that measures radiation exposure, and records are kept of total exposure accumulated over time. Other routine precautions include the use of safety devices (such as lead aprons, lead gloves, and other shielding) and the use of disposable gowns, gloves, and masks. Careful attention to safety procedures has greatly reduced or eliminated radiation hazards for the technologist.

Radiologic technology is dedicated to conserving life and health. Technologists derive satisfaction from their work, which helps promote health and alleviate human suffering. Those who specialize in radiation therapy need to be able to handle the close relationships they inevitably develop while working with very sick or dying people over a period of time.

OUTLOOK

Overall, employment for radiologic technologists is expected to grow faster than the average through 2010, according to the U.S. Department of Labor. The demand for qualified technologists in some areas of the country far exceeds the supply. This shortage is particularly acute in rural areas and small towns. Those who are willing to relocate to these areas may have increased job prospects. Radiologic technologists who are trained to do more than one type of imaging procedure will also find that they have increased job opportunities. Finally, those specializing in sonography are predicted to have more opportunities than those working only with radiographs. One reason for this is ultrasound's increasing popularity due to its lack of possible side effects.

In the years to come, increasing numbers of radiologic technologists will be employed in nonhospital settings, such as physicians' offices, clinics, health maintenance organizations, laboratories, government agencies, and diagnostic imaging centers. This pattern will be part of the overall trend toward lowering health care costs by delivering more care outside of hospitals. Nevertheless, hospitals will remain the major employers of radiologic technologists for the near future. Because of the increasing importance of radiologic technology in the diagnosis and treatment of disease, it is unlikely that hospitals will do fewer radiologic procedures than in the past. Instead, they try to do more on an outpatient basis and on weekends and evenings. This should increase the demand for part-time technologists and thus open more opportunities for flexible work schedules.

FOR MORE INFORMATION

For information on certification and educational programs, contact
American Registry of Radiologic Technologists
1255 Northland Drive
St. Paul, MN 55120-1155
Tel: 651-687-0048
http://www.arrt.org

For information about the field, a catalog of educational products, and to access their job bank, contact
American Society of Radiologic Technologists
15000 Central Avenue, SE
Albuquerque, NM 87123-3917
Tel: 800-444-2778
http://www.asrt.org

For an educational resource guide, contact
Society of Diagnostic Medical Sonography
2745 Dallas Parkway, Suite 350
Plano, TX 75093-8730
Tel: 800-229-9506
http://www.sdms.org

For career and education information, contact
Canadian Association of Medical Radiation Technologists
1510-130 Albert Street
Ottawa, ON K1P 5G4 Canada
Tel: 613-234-0012
http://www.camrt.ca

Respiratory Therapists and Technicians

OVERVIEW

Respiratory therapists, also known as *respiratory care practitioners*, evaluate, treat, and care for patients with deficiencies or abnormalities of the cardiopulmonary (heart/lung) system, either providing temporary relief from chronic ailments or administering emergency care where life is threatened. They are involved with the supervision of other respiratory care workers in their area of treatment. *Respiratory technicians* have many of the same responsibilities as therapists; however, technicians do not supervise other respiratory care workers.

Working under a physician's direction, these workers set up and operate respirators, mechanical ventilators, and other devices. They monitor the functioning of the equipment and the patients' response to the therapy and maintain the patients' charts. They also assist patients with breathing exercises, and inspect, test, and order repairs for respiratory therapy equipment. They may demonstrate procedures to trainees and other health care personnel. Approximately 110,000 respiratory therapy workers are employed in the United States.

HISTORY

In normal respiration, the chest muscles and the diaphragm (a muscular disk that separates the chest and abdominal cavities) draw in air by expanding the chest volume. When this automatic response is impaired because of illness or injury, artificial means must be applied to keep the patient breathing and to prevent brain damage or death. Respiratory problems can result from many conditions. For example, with bronchial asthma, the bronchial tubes are narrowed by spasmodic contractions, and they produce an excessive amount of mucus. Emphysema is a disease in which the lungs lose their elasticity. Diseases of the central nervous system and drug poisoning may result in paralysis, which could lead to suffocation. Emergency conditions such as heart failure, stroke, drowning, or shock also interfere with the normal breathing process.

Respirators, or ventilators, are mechanical devices that enable patients with cardiorespiratory problems to breathe. The original "iron lung" was designed in 1937 by Philip Drinker and Louise A. Shaw, of the Harvard School of Public Health in Boston, primarily to treat people with polio. It was a cylindrical machine that enclosed the patient's entire body, except the head. This type of respirator is still in use today. The newer ventilators, however, are much smaller, dome-shaped breastplates that wrap around the patient's chest and allow more freedom of motion. Other sophisticated, complex equipment to aid patients with breathing difficulties includes mechanical ventilators, apparatuses that administer therapeutic gas, environmental control systems, and aerosol generators.

Respiratory therapists and technicians and their assistants are the workers who operate this equipment and administer care and life support to patients suffering from respiratory problems.

THE JOB

Respiratory therapists and technicians treat patients with various cardiorespiratory problems. They may provide care that affords temporary relief from chronic illnesses such as asthma or emphysema, or they may administer life-support treatment to victims of heart failure, stroke, drowning, or shock. These specialists often mean the difference between life and death in cases involving acute respiratory conditions, as may result from head injuries or drug poisoning. Adults who stop breathing for longer than three to five minutes rarely survive without serious brain damage, and an absence of respiratory activity for more than nine minutes almost always results in death. Respiratory therapists carry out their duties under a physician's direction and supervision. Technicians typically work under the supervision of a respiratory therapist and physician, following specific instructions. Therapists and technicians set up and operate special devices to treat patients who need temporary or emergency relief from breathing difficulties. The equipment may include respirators, positive-pressure breathing machines, or environmental control systems. Aerosol inhalants are administered to confine medication to the lungs. Respiratory therapists often treat patients who have undergone surgery because anesthesia depresses normal respiration, thus the patients need some support to restore their full breathing capability and to prevent respiratory illnesses.

In evaluating patients, therapists test the capacity of the lungs and analyze the oxygen and carbon dioxide concentration and potential of hydrogen (pH), a measure of the acidity or alkalinity level of the blood. To measure lung capacity, therapists have patients breathe into an instrument that measures the volume and flow of air during inhalation and exhalation. By comparing the reading with the norm for the patient's age, height, weight, and gender, respiratory therapists can determine whether lung deficiencies exist. To analyze oxygen, carbon dioxide, and pH levels, therapists draw an arterial blood sample, place it in a blood gas analyzer, and relay the results to a physician.

Respiratory therapists watch equipment gauges and maintain prescribed volumes of oxygen or other inhalants. Besides monitoring the equipment to be sure it is operating properly, they observe the patient's physiological response to the therapy and consult with physicians in case of any adverse reactions. They also record pertinent identification and therapy information on each patient's chart and keep records of the cost of materials and the charges to the patients.

Therapists instruct patients and their families on how to use respiratory equipment at home, and they may demonstrate respiratory therapy procedures to trainees and other health care personnel. Their responsibilities include inspecting and testing equipment. If it is faulty, they either make minor repairs themselves or order major repairs.

Respiratory therapy workers include therapists, technicians, and assistants. Differences between respiratory therapists' duties and those of other respiratory care workers' include supervising technicians and assistants, teaching new staff, and bearing primary responsibility for the care given in their areas. At times the respiratory therapist may need to work independently and make clinical judgments on the type of care to be given to a patient. Although technicians can perform many of the same activities as a therapist (for example, monitoring equipment, checking patient responses, and giving medicine), they do not make independent decisions about what type of care to give. Respiratory assistants clean, sterilize, store, and generally take care of the equipment but have very little contact with patients.

REQUIREMENTS

High School

To prepare for this field while you are still in high school, take health and science classes, including biology, chemistry, and physics. Mathematics and statistics classes will also be useful to you since much of this work involves using numbers and making calculations. Take computer science courses to become familiar with using technical and complex equipment and to become familiar with programs you can use to document your work. Since some of your responsibilities may include working directly with patients to teach them therapies, take English classes to improve your communication skills. Studying a foreign language may also be useful.

Postsecondary Training

Formal training is necessary for entry to this field. Training is offered at the postsecondary level by hospitals, medical schools, colleges and universities, trade schools, vocational-technical institutes, and the armed forces. The Committee on Accreditation for Respiratory Care (CoARC) has accredited more than 400 programs nationwide. A listing of these programs is available on CoARC's website, http://www.coarc.com. To be eligible for a respiratory therapy program, you must have graduated from high school.

Accredited respiratory therapy programs combine class work with clinical work. Programs vary in length, depending on the degree awarded. A certificate program generally takes one year to complete, an associate's degree usually takes two years, and a bachelor's degree program typically takes four years. In addition, it is important to note that some programs (known as "advanced-level") will prepare you for becoming a registered respiratory therapist (RRT), while other programs (known as "entry-level") will prepare you for becoming a certified respiratory therapist (CRT). RRT-prepared graduates will be eligible for jobs as respiratory therapists once they have been certified. CRT-prepared graduates, on the other hand, are only eligible for jobs as respiratory technicians after certification. The areas of study for both therapists and technicians cover human anatomy and physiology, chemistry, physics, microbiology, and mathematics. Technical studies include courses such as patient evaluation, respiratory care pharmacology, pulmonary diseases, and care procedures.

There are no standard hiring requirements for assistants. Department heads in charge of hiring set the standards and may require only a high school diploma.

Certification and Licensing

The National Board for Respiratory Care (NBRC) offers voluntary certification to graduates of CoARC-accredited programs. The certifications, as previously mentioned, are registered respiratory therapist (RRT) and certified respiratory therapist (CRT). You must have at least an associate's degree to be eligible to take the CRT exam. Anyone desiring certification must take the CRT exam first. After successfully completing this exam, those who are eligible can take the RRT exam. CRTs who meet further education and experience requirements can qualify for the RRT credential.

Certification is highly recommended because most employers require this credential. Those who are designated CRT or are eligible to take the exam are qualified for technician jobs that are entry-level or generalist positions. Employers usually require those with supervisory positions or those in intensive care specialties to have the RRT (or RRT eligibility).

More than 40 states regulate respiratory care personnel through licensing or certification. Requirements vary, so you will need to check with your state's regulatory board for specific information. The NBRC website provides helpful contact information for state licensure agencies at http://www.nbrc.org/StateLicensureMenu.htm.

Other Requirements

Respiratory therapists must enjoy working with people. You must be sensitive to your patients' physical and psychological needs because you will be dealing with people who may be in pain or who may be frightened. The work of this occupational group is of great significance. Respiratory therapists are often responsible for the lives and well-being of people already in critical condition. You must pay strict attention to detail, be able to follow instructions and work as part of a team, and remain cool in emergencies. Mechanical ability and manual dexterity are necessary to operate much of the respiratory equipment.

EXPLORING

Those considering advanced study may obtain a list of accredited educational programs in respiratory therapy by writing to the American Association for Respiratory Care at the address listed at the end of this article. Formal training in this field is available in hospitals, vocational-technical institutes, private trade schools, and other noncollegiate settings as well. Local hospitals can provide information on training opportunities. School vocational counselors may be sources of additional information about educational matters and may be able to set up interviews with or lectures by a respiratory therapy practitioner from a local hospital.

Hospitals are excellent places to obtain part-time and summer employment. They have a continuing need for helpers in many departments. Even though the work may not be directly related to respiratory therapy, you will gain knowledge of the operation of a hospital and may be in a position to get acquainted with respiratory therapists and observe them as they carry out their duties. If part-time or temporary work is not available, you may wish to volunteer your services.

EMPLOYERS

More than four out of five respiratory therapy jobs were in hospital departments of respiratory care, anesthesiology, or pulmonary medicine. The rest are employed by oxygen equipment rental companies, ambulance services, nursing homes, home health agencies, and physicians' offices.

STARTING OUT

Graduates of CoARC-accredited respiratory therapy training programs may use their school's placement offices to help them find jobs. Otherwise, they may apply directly to the individual local health care facilities.

High school graduates may apply directly to local hospitals for jobs as respiratory therapy assistants. If your goal is to become a therapist or technician, however, you will need to enroll in a formal respiratory therapy educational program.

ADVANCEMENT

Many respiratory therapists start out as assistants or technicians. With appropriate training courses and experience, they advance to the therapist level. Respiratory therapists with sufficient experience may be promoted to assistant chief or chief therapist. With graduate education, they may be qualified to teach respiratory therapy at the college level or move into administrative positions such as director.

EARNINGS

Respiratory therapists earned a median salary of $37,680 in 2000, according to the *Occupational Outlook Handbook*. The lowest 10 percent earned less than $28,620, and the highest 10 percent earned more than $50,660. Median annual earnings of respiratory therapy technicians were $32,860 in 2000. Salaries ranged from less than $22,830 to more than $46,800.

According to findings from AARC's 2000 *Respiratory Therapist Human Resources Survey,* those in staff positions reported a mean wage of $16.66 per hour, which equals approximately $34,650 annually for full-time work. Those holding positions as supervisors reported a mean hourly wage of $20.99 (approximately $43,660 per year). And those in director positions had a mean hourly wage of $26.45, which works out to approximately $55,015 annually.

Hospital workers receive benefits that include health insurance, paid vacations and sick leave, and pension plans. Some institutions provide additional benefits, such as uniforms and parking, and offer free courses or tuition reimbursement for job-related courses.

WORK ENVIRONMENT

Respiratory therapists generally work in extremely clean, quiet surroundings. They usually work 40 hours a week, which may include nights and weekends because hospitals are in operation 24 hours a day, seven days a week. The work requires long hours of standing and may be very stressful during emergencies.

A possible hazard is that the inhalants these employees work with are highly flammable. The danger of fire is minimized, however, if the workers test equipment regularly and are strict about taking safety precautions. As do workers in many other health occupations, respiratory therapists run a risk of catching infectious diseases. Careful adherence to proper procedures minimizes the risk.

OUTLOOK

Employment growth for respiratory therapists is expected to be more rapid than the average for all occupations through 2010, despite the fact that efforts to control rising health care costs has reduced the number of job opportunities in hospitals.

The increasing demand for therapists is the result of several factors. The fields of neonatal care and gerontology are growing. Also, there is a greater incidence of cardiopulmonary and AIDS-related diseases, coupled with more advanced methods of diagnosing and treating them.

Employment opportunities for respiratory therapists and technicians should be very favorable in the rapidly growing field of home health care, although this area accounts for only a small number of respiratory therapy jobs. In addition to jobs in home health agencies and hospital-based home health programs, there should be numerous openings for respiratory therapists in equipment rental companies and in firms that provide respiratory care on a contract basis.

FOR MORE INFORMATION

For information on scholarships, continuing education, job listings, and careers in respiratory therapy, contact
American Association for Respiratory Care
11030 Ables Lane
Dallas, TX 75229
Tel: 972-243-2272
Email: info@aarc.org
http://www.aarc.org

For more information on allied health care careers as well as a listing of accredited programs, contact
Commission on Accreditation of Allied Health Education
    Programs
35 East Wacker Drive, Suite 1970
Chicago, IL 60601-2208
Tel: 312-553-9355
Email: caahep@caahep.org
http://www.caahep.org

For a list of CoARC-accredited training programs, contact
Committee on Accreditation for Respiratory Care (CoARC)
1248 Harwood Road
Bedford, TX 76021-4244
Tel: 817-283-2835
Email: info@coarc.com
http://www.coarc.com

For information on licensing and certification, contact
National Board for Respiratory Care
8310 Nieman Road
Lenexa, KS 66214-1579
Tel: 913-599-4200
Email: nbrc-info@nbrc.org
http://www.nbrc.org

INTERVIEW

Thomas Johnson, MS, RRT, is the program director of the division of respiratory care at Long Island University's School of Health Professions. He spoke with the editors of Careers in Focus: Medical Technicians *about his career path and the field of respiratory care.*

Q. How long have you been in your current position? What other jobs have you held in this field?

A. I have been with the university for nearly 10 years and in the field of respiratory care since 1973. I have been a staff therapist (United Hospital, NYU Medical Center, and Brookdale Hospital), a supervisor (Brookdale Hospital), an instructor in the NYU-Bellevue Hospital respiratory therapy program, and an assistant director of respiratory care at Cabrini Medical Center. For eight years I was the director of respiratory care and pulmonary services at Clara Maass Medical Center. I have also worked in home care and in medical sales.

Q. What is your typical workday like?

A. A typical workday is about 10 hours long. It may include three or more hours of classroom and/or laboratory instruction for three classes per week. My day will include interaction with university administration at some level, formal and informal meetings with faculty and students, and record keeping. It may include recruiting new students, presentations to faculty, student groups, or visitors, and investigating technological applications for the classroom, laboratory, or clinical field experience. While I rarely see patients, I do research on exercise physiology, medical responses to biological and chemical terrorism, and on developing effective medical education for students and the public.

Q. What is your work environment like?

A. We are fortunate to have a well-designed and well-equipped health science building with excellent computer information systems. Most of my work is in a classroom or laboratory, however, to do research I have to go to the subject. For instance, to study exercise-induced asthma I have worked in the gym or athletic field.

Most respiratory therapists work in acute care hospitals, as I did. Our patients range in age from premature babies to people who were born at the turn of the 20th century. We take care of toddlers and basketball players. Our patients may have a long-standing disease or suffered a severe accident. Hospital work is tough but rewarding.

Q. What were your expectations entering this field? Are they much different from the realities?

A. When I entered the field in 1973, the scope of respiratory practice was undergoing rapid expansion. I thought that I would be working with asthmatics, emphysemic patients, and heart attack patients that are adults and children. At United Hospital I worked with newborns and premature newborns and found it fascinating. The realities were better than I expected. As with any profession there were peaks and valleys—the good thing is that the valleys were not so deep or long.

Q. What kind of education and training did you pursue for your career?

A. In my current position I needed formal education, which required me to have a master's degree (mine is in exercise physiology) and a minimum of two years full-time teaching (mine was with NYU Bellevue Hospital's Respiratory Care program) and managerial experience.

The individual who wishes to become a respiratory therapist must have at least an associate's degree in respiratory therapy or respiratory care and pass the National Board for Respiratory Care's certified respiratory therapist examination. He or she then must obtain a state license to practice. Continued professional growth will require a bachelor's degree or more.

Q. Did you complete any internships or clinical practice to help you prepare for your career?

A. All health professions require that the student participate in a lengthy clinical field experience; mine was no exception. The tradition of combining classroom-laboratory-real hospital experience is vital to create a good clinician. This provides the student with real-world experience and starts the student in networking for their first and future jobs.

Q. What is the best way to find a job in this field?

A. As with most, a good network of people who will guide you is essential. However, there are also good sources in professional journals (such as *AARC Times* and *ADVANCE for Respiratory Care Practitioners*), in newspapers, and online.

Q. What would you say are the most important skills and personal qualities for someone in your field?

A. Respiratory therapists tend to be people who like to solve mysteries, have good interpersonal skills, and enjoy interacting with people and technology. Respiratory therapists must be able to deal calmly with crisis, have good hand-eye coordination, and be well spoken. Of course, they must have scientific knowledge and be able to translate that knowledge into action.

Q. What advice would you give to someone who is interested in pursuing this type of career?

A. Volunteer with your local lung, heart, or cystic fibrosis societies, March of Dimes Association, or chapter of the American Cancer Society. Learn first aid and CPR and consider working or volunteering with a local ambulance corps. Visit the American Association for Respiratory Care's website (http://www.aarc.org) and visit a college program in your vicinity.

   If you are concerned with burnout or boredom on the job, then a career in medicine is the antidote. In respiratory care, you can re-invent your career as many times as you wish.

Special Procedures Technologists

OVERVIEW

Special procedures technologists are trained individuals who operate medical diagnostic imaging equipment such as computer tomography (CT) and magnetic resonance imaging (MRI) scanners, and assist in imaging procedures such as angiography and cardiac catheterization (CC). They are employed in various health care settings such as hospitals, clinics, and imaging centers. Their skills will continue to be in high demand as the population ages and cancer and heart disease continue to be major health concerns.

HISTORY

Advances in medical technology have resulted in more sophisticated patient testing using more complex equipment. As this technology has become more sophisticated, the need for trained personnel to assist physicians and specially trained technologists to operate this equipment became apparent. In addition, trained personnel became essential to perform and document the testing procedures, as well as to assist with the patients. The special procedures technologist career field evolved from this need. Technologists are trained to understand the operation of some of the testing equipment and to assist medical personnel as they perform these tests. They are also taught how to position patients during the testing and how to deal with any fears and anxieties they might have during the procedures.

THE JOB

Special procedures technologists' duties vary depending on the training they have with specific diagnostic equipment and testing procedures. Job requirements also vary with the degree of assistance required for certain testing and diagnostic procedures.

Special procedures technologists may assist radiologic technologists with positioning a patient for examination, immobilizing them, preparing the equipment, and monitoring the equipment and patient's progress during the procedure. An *angiographer* is a special procedures technologist who assists with a procedure called an angiogram, which shows any changes that may have occurred to the blood vessels of the patient's circulatory system. The special procedures technologist may assist with many aspects of this test. Similarly, some special procedures technologists may assist cardiologists with the invasive procedure called cardiac catheterization by positioning the patients and explaining to them the procedures performed. They may also monitor and document the patients' vital signs such as blood pressure and respiration and enter that information directly into a computer that controls testing procedures. Some special procedures technologists assist with CT scanning (also known as CAT scanning), which combines X rays with computer technology to create clear, cross-section images that provide more details than standard X rays, with minimal radiation exposure. The *CT technologist* might

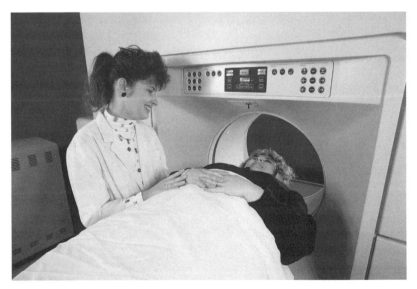

A special procedures technologist reassures a patient who is about to undergo a CAT scan. (*Corbis*)

enter data into the scanner's computer control, which includes the type of scan to be performed, the time required, and the thickness of the cross section. The technologist might also observe and reassure the patient while the testing procedure is performed. Another imaging procedure called MRI produces the most detailed and flexible images among the various imaging techniques. A special procedures technologist often assists with this procedure by explaining the test to the patient and making certain that the patient is not carrying any metal objects that could be hazardous to the patient during the test and could also damage the equipment. The *MRI technologist* might enter the necessary data, such as patient information, the orientation of the scan, and the part of the body to be scanned into the computer. The technologist might initiate the scan and observe the patient through a window in the control room and on a closed-circuit video display, while maintaining voice contact and reassuring the patient.

REQUIREMENTS

High School

High school classes that will help you prepare for further education as a special procedures technologist include advanced courses in anatomy, physiology, and math. Science courses, including biology, chemistry, and physics, are also helpful. Classes in communication such as speech and English, and classes that reinforce written and verbal skills are also helpful. Because most imaging specialties depend heavily on computer technology, you should gain a good understanding of the use of computers. Studies regarding various cultures will also help you deal with patients from various backgrounds. In addition, you might consider studying a foreign language, with the idea of being able to communicate with patients whose understanding of English is not strong.

Postsecondary Training

The most common way to enter this field is to get an associate's degree in radiology. Some people choose to get a bachelor's degree, but this route is mainly for those interested in going into administrative or teaching positions. Associate programs can be found at community colleges, vocational and technical training schools, or in the military. When deciding on which program to attend, look for those accredited by the Joint Review Committee on Education in Radiologic Technology; a degree from an accredited school will aid you in your job search. Your course of study will include both classroom instruction and clinical experience. Courses will cover topics such as medical terminology, medical ethics, radiation physics, and positioning of patients. In all cases, special procedures technologists must complete additional training, usually offered through a hospital, medical center, college, or vocational or technical training school, in their specialty area.

Certification or Licensing

Graduates of accredited programs are eligible to take the four-hour certification examination offered by the American Registry of Radiologic Technologists. Although certification is voluntary, it is highly recommended since many employers will only hire certified technologists.

Licensing requirements for radiologic technologists vary by state, although most states and Puerto Rico do require some form of licensing. The American Society of Radiologic Technologists (ASRT) has general information on state requirements and also notes that licensure legislation is under consideration in several states (see the end of this article for ASRT's contact information). You will need to contact your state's licensing board for specific information about requirements in your area.

Other Requirements

You should have an interest in medicine and compassion for patients to be a successful special procedures technologist. You should have an aptitude for science and math and have strong communication skills. In addition, you should be conscientious, responsible, efficient, and have the ability to work under stress and in emergency situations. You should also work well with people, both independently and as a part of a team. Manual dexterity and stamina are also required. Many employers also require technicians to have up-to-date cardiopulmonary resuscitation (CPR) training.

EXPLORING

If you are interested in entering the health care field, you can begin your involvement while still in high school. Most hospitals, nursing homes, mental health centers, and other treatment facilities have volunteer programs that allow you to explore the health care environment and gain insight into medicine and patient care. You may be able to get a paid part-time or summer position working as a nurse's aide or home health care helper. In addition to these possibilities, ask your school counselor or a science teacher to help you arrange for a special procedures technologist to give a career talk to interested students. You may also be able to meet a special procedures technologist by contacting a local hospital or imaging center and asking for an informational interview with this person. Another possibility is to ask if you can spend part of a day "shadowing" the individual at the workplace.

EMPLOYERS

Special procedures technologists are employed in a variety of health care settings. Hospitals are the most likely source for employment, especially for techniques such as CT and MRI scanning, which require costly equipment. Health maintenance organizations and other health care clinics and centers also hire personnel trained to carry out the variety of testing procedures needed for medical care. Diagnostic imaging centers that are specifically dedicated to performing special imaging procedures are also likely employers. Also, the U.S. government employs radiologic and other imaging personnel, usually through the Department of Veterans Affairs or as members of the armed forces.

STARTING OUT

Most special procedures technologists begin their careers as radiology technologists and then receive additional training in their special procedure. Many technologists find employment through their school's placement service. Some trade journals and area newspapers also list job opportunities. Applying directly to health care and imaging facilities may also produce results.

ADVANCEMENT

Advancement in special procedures fields is generally limited as these specialties already represent advanced areas of radiology. With experience, however, a special procedures technologist may advance to greater responsibilities and to supervisory positions. Some people advance in this field by completing a bachelor's degree in radiology and moving into administrative or teaching positions. In addition, special procedures work may be a valuable bridge to a more advanced medical career, such as a doctor. Skills of a special procedures technologist are in demand in the United States and other countries as well, so there is a possibility of travel to, or employment in, other countries that recognize U.S. training and certification.

EARNINGS

Salaries for the different branches of special imaging procedures vary by type of procedure, geographic location, type of employer, and experience level. According to recruiting company Health Care Job Store, annual salaries for special procedures technicians can range from a low of $14,000 to a high of $60,000. A September 2000 article in the *Chicago Tribune* reported that MRI technicians had yearly earnings ranging from $38,000 to $60,000. The U.S. Department of Labor found that the median annual salary of all radiologic technologists was $36,000 in 2000.

Benefits vary widely. Most benefit packages, however, include paid vacation and holidays, as well as sick leave, and medical and dental insurance. Some employers may offer additional benefits such as on-site day care and tuition reimbursement.

WORK ENVIRONMENT

Special procedures technologists usually work in one of several departments within a hospital or medical testing facility or clinic. These departments have rooms set up to perform specific tests, such as cardiac catheterization, MRIs, or CAT scans. The testing is usually done as part of a medical team; however, some of the setup may have to be done independently, so technologists may be required to make critical decisions.

Daily schedules and shifts may vary according to the size of the hospital, the number of patients requiring testing, and the type of imaging techniques performed. Although a technologist may be scheduled to work an eight-hour shift, the health care environment is often unpredictable and longer hours may be required. Because technologists deal with sick and dying people, and medical personnel are often required to make life and death decisions, the job can be quite stressful.

OUTLOOK

Employment for radiologic technologists—including those with credentials and specialized knowledge to perform special procedures—will grow faster than the average through 2010, according to the U.S. Department of Labor. As the population ages and heart disease and cancer continue to be among the primary health concerns in the United States, there will continue to be a high demand for skilled technologists who can assist in the diagnosis, prevention, and treatment of these and other conditions. Also, as more and more sophisticated testing and imaging procedures are developed, and as new techniques become available, the demand for skilled special procedures technologists to operate, perform, and assist in these procedures will continue to grow.

FOR MORE INFORMATION

For information on special procedures technologists careers, accredited schools, and certification, contact the following organizations:

American Registry of Radiologic Technologists
1255 Northland Drive
St. Paul, MN 55120-1155
Tel: 651-687-0048
http://www.arrt.org

American Society of Radiologic Technologists
15000 Central Avenue, SE
Albuquerque, NM 87123-3917
Tel: 800-444-2778
http://www.asrt.org

Joint Review Committee on Education in Radiologic Technology
20 North Wacker Drive, Suite 900
Chicago, IL 60606-2901
Tel: 312-704-5300
Email: mail@jrcert.org
http://www.jrcert.org

Surgical Technologists

OVERVIEW

Surgical technologists, also called *surgical technicians* or *operating room technicians,* are members of the surgical team who work in the operating room with surgeons, nurses, anesthesiologists, and other personnel before, during, and after surgery. They perform functions that ensure a safe and sterile environment. To prepare a patient for surgery, they may wash, shave, and disinfect the area where the incision will be made. They arrange the equipment, instruments, and supplies in the operating room according to the preference of the surgeons and nurses. During the operation, they adjust lights and other equipment as needed. They count sponges, needles, and instruments used during the operation, hand instruments and supplies to the surgeon, and hold retractors and cut sutures as directed. They maintain specified supplies of fluids (for example, saline, plasma, blood, and glucose), and may assist in administering these fluids. Following the operation, they may clean and restock the operating room and wash and sterilize the used equipment using germicides, autoclaves, and sterilizers. There are approximately 71,000 surgical technologists employed in the United States.

HISTORY

While the origins of surgery go back to prehistoric times, two scientific developments made modern surgery possible. The first was the discovery of anesthesia in the mid-19th century. Because the anesthesia eliminated the patient's pain, surgeons were able to take their time during operations, enabling them to try more complex procedures.

The second important discovery was that of the causes of infection. Until Louis Pasteur's discovery of germs and Joseph Lister's development of aseptic surgery in the 19th century, so many people died of infection after operations that the value of surgery was extremely limited.

During World War II, the profession of surgical technology grew when there was a critical need for assistance in performing surgical procedures and a shortage of qualified personnel. Shortly after, formal educational programs were started to teach these medical professionals.

Throughout the last century, the nature of most surgical procedures, with all of their sophisticated techniques for monitoring and safeguarding the patient's condition, has become so complex that more and more people are required to assist the surgeon or surgeons. While many of the tasks that are performed during the operation require highly trained professionals with many years of education, there are also simpler, more standardized tasks that require people with less complex training and skills. Over the years, such tasks have been taken care of by people referred to as orderlies, scrub nurses, and surgical orderlies.

Today, such people are referred to as surgical technologists, operating room technicians, or surgical technicians. For the most part, these medical professionals have received specialized training in a community college, vocational or technical school, or a hospital-sponsored program. They are eligible to earn certificates of competence, and, in general, enjoy a higher degree of professional status and recognition than did their predecessors.

THE JOB

Surgical technologists are health professionals who work in the surgical suite with surgeons, anesthesiologists, registered nurses, and other surgical personnel delivering surgical patient care.

In general, the work responsibilities of surgical technologists may be divided into three phases: preoperative (before surgery), intraoperative (during surgery), and postoperative (after surgery). Surgical technologists may work as the *scrub person, circulator,* or *surgical first assistant*.

In the preoperative phase, surgical technologists prepare the operating room by selecting and opening sterile supplies such as drapes, sutures, sponges, electrosurgical devices, suction tubing, and surgical instruments. They assemble, adjust, and check nonsterile equipment to ensure that it is in proper working order. Surgical technologists also operate sterilizers, lights, suction machines, electrosurgical units, and diagnostic equipment.

When patients arrive in the surgical suite, surgical technologists may assist in preparing them for surgery by providing physical and emotional support, checking charts, and observing vital signs. They properly position the patient on the operating table, assist in connecting and applying surgical equipment and monitoring devices, and prepare the incision site by cleansing the skin with an antiseptic solution.

During surgery, surgical technologists have primary responsibility for maintaining the sterile field. They constantly watch that all members of the team adhere to aseptic techniques so the patient does not develop a postoperative infection. As the scrub person, they most often function as the sterile member of the surgical team who passes instruments, sutures, and sponges during surgery. After "scrubbing," which involves the thorough cleansing of the hands and forearms, they put on a sterile gown and gloves and prepare the sterile instruments and supplies that will be needed. After other members of the sterile team have scrubbed, they assist them with gowning and gloving and applying sterile drapes around the operative site.

Surgical technologists must anticipate the needs of surgeons during the procedure, passing instruments and providing sterile items in an efficient manner. Checking, mixing, and dispensing appropriate fluids and drugs in the sterile field are other common tasks. They share with the circulator the responsibility for accounting for sponges, needles, and instruments before, during, and after surgery. They may hold retractors or instruments, sponge or suction the operative site, or cut suture material as directed by the surgeon. They connect drains and tubing and receive and prepare specimens for subsequent pathologic analysis.

Surgical technologists most often function as the scrub person, but may function in the nonsterile role of circulator. The circulator does not wear a sterile gown and gloves, but is available to assist the surgical team. As a circulator, the surgical technologist obtains additional supplies or equipment, assists the anesthesiologist, keeps a written account of the surgical procedure, and assists the scrub person.

Surgical first assistants, those technologists with additional education or training, provide aid in retracting tissue, controlling bleeding, and other technical functions that help surgeons during the procedure.

After surgery, surgical technologists are responsible for preparing and applying dressings, including plaster or synthetic casting materials, and for preparing the operating room for the next patient. They may provide staffing in postoperative recovery rooms where patients' responses are carefully monitored in the critical phases following general anesthesia.

Some of these responsibilities vary, depending on the size of the hospital and department in which the surgical technologist works;

they also vary based on geographic location and health care needs of the local community.

REQUIREMENTS

High School

During your high school years, you should take courses that develop your basic skills in mathematics, science, and English. You also should take all available courses in health and biology.

Postsecondary Training

Surgical technology education is available through postsecondary programs offered by community and junior colleges, vocational and technical schools, the military, universities, and structured hospital programs in surgical technology. A high school diploma is required for entry into any of these programs.

More than 350 of these programs are accredited by the Commission on Accreditation of Allied Health Education Programs (CAAHEP). The accredited programs vary from nine to 12 months for a diploma or certificate to two years for an associate's degree. You can expect to take courses in medical terminology, communications, anatomy, physiology, microbiology, pharmacology, medical ethics, and legal responsibilities. You gain a thorough knowledge of patient preparation and care, surgical procedures, surgical instruments and equipment, and principles of asepsis (how to prevent infection). In addition to classroom learning, you receive intensive supervised clinical experience in local hospitals, which is an important component of your education.

Certification or Licensing

Increasing numbers of hospitals are requiring certification as a condition of employment. Surgical technologists may earn a professional credential by passing a nationally administered certifying examination. To take the examination, you must be currently or previously certified or be a graduate of a CAAHEP-accredited program. The Liaison Council on Certification for the Surgical Technologist (LCC-ST), an independent affiliate of the Association of Surgical Technologists, is the certifying agency for the profession. Those who pass the exam and fulfill education and experience requirements are granted the designation of certified surgical technologist (CST). To renew the six-year certificate, the CST must earn continuing education credits or retake the certifying examination. The LCC-ST also offers an advanced credential for surgical first assistants; this exam awards the designation of CST certified first assistant (CST/CFA).

Other Requirements

Surgical technologists must possess an educational background in the medical sciences, a strong sense of responsibility, a concern for order, and an ability to integrate a number of tasks at the same time. You need good manual dexterity to handle awkward surgical instruments with speed and agility. In addition, you need physical stamina to stand through long surgical procedures.

EXPLORING

It is difficult to gain any direct experience on a part-time basis in surgical technology. The first opportunities for direct experience generally come in the clinical and laboratory phases of your educational programs. However, interested students can explore some aspects of this career in several ways. You or your teachers can arrange a visit to a hospital, clinic, or other surgical setting in order to learn about the work. You also can visit a school with a CAAHEP-accredited program. During such a visit, you can discuss career plans with the admissions counselor. In addition, volunteering at a local hospital or nursing home can give you insight into the health care environment and help you evaluate your aptitude to work in such a setting.

EMPLOYERS

Most surgical technologists are employed in hospital operating rooms, clinics, and surgicenters. They also work in delivery rooms, cast rooms, emergency departments, ambulatory care areas, and central supply departments. Surgical technologists may also be employed directly by surgeons as private scrubs or as surgical first assistants.

STARTING OUT

Graduates of programs are often offered jobs in the same hospital in which they received their clinical training. Programs usually cooperate closely with hospitals in the area, which are usually eager to employ technologists educated in local programs. Available positions are also advertised in newspaper want ads.

ADVANCEMENT

With increased experience, surgical technologists can serve in management roles in surgical services departments and may work as central service managers, surgery schedulers, and materials managers.

The role of surgical first assistant on the surgical team requires additional training and experience and is considered an advanced role.

Surgical technologists function well in a number of diverse areas, as evidenced by their employment in organ and tissue procurement/preservation, cardiac catheterization laboratories, medical sales and research, and medical-legal auditing for insurance companies. A number are instructors and directors of surgical technology programs.

EARNINGS

Salaries vary greatly in different institutions and localities. According to the *Occupational Outlook Handbook,* the average salary for surgical technologists was $29,020 in 2000, but ranged from $20,490 to $40,310 a year (excluding overtime). Some technologists with experience earn much more. Most surgical technologists are required to be periodically on call—available to work on short notice in cases of emergency—and can earn overtime from such work. Graduates of educational programs usually receive salaries higher than technologists without formal education. In general, technologists working on the East Coast and West Coast earn more than surgical technologists in other parts of the country. Surgical first assistants and private scrubs employed directly by surgeons tend to earn more than surgical technologists employed by hospitals.

WORK ENVIRONMENT

Surgical technologists naturally spend most of their time in the operating room. Operating rooms are cool, well lighted, orderly, and extremely clean. Technologists are often required to be on their feet for long intervals during which their attention must be closely focused on the operation.

Members of the surgical team, including surgical technologists, wear sterile gowns, gloves, caps, masks, and eye protection. This surgical attire is meant not only to protect the patient from infection but also to protect the surgical team from any infection or bloodborne diseases that the patient may have. Surgery is usually performed during the day; however, hospitals, clinics, and other facilities require 24-hour-a-day coverage. Most surgical technologists work regular 40-hour weeks, although many are required to be periodically on call.

Surgical technologists must be able to work under great pressure in stressful situations. The need for surgery is often a matter of life and death, and one can never assume that procedures will go as planned. If operations do not go well, nerves may fray and tempers flare. Technologists must understand that this is the result of stressful conditions and should not take this anger personally.

In addition, surgical technologists should have a strong desire to help others. Surgery is performed on people, not machines. Patients literally entrust their lives to the surgical team, and they rely on them to treat them in a dignified and professional manner. Individuals with these characteristics find surgical technology a rewarding career in which they can make an important contribution to the health and well-being of their community.

OUTLOOK

According to the U.S. Department of Labor, the field of surgical technology is projected to experience rapid job growth through 2010. Population growth, longevity, and improvement in medical and surgical procedures have all contributed to a growing demand for surgical services and hence for surgical technologists. As long as the rate at which people undergo surgery continues to increase, there will continue to be a need for this profession. Also, as surgical methods become increasingly complex, more surgical technologists will likely be needed.

An increasing number of surgical procedures are being performed in the offices of physicians and ambulatory surgical centers, requiring the skills of surgical technologists. As a result, employment for technologists in these non hospital settings should grow much faster than the average.

FOR MORE INFORMATION

For information on education programs and certification, contact the following organizations:

Association of Surgical Technologists
7108-C South Alton Way
Centennial, CO 80112
Tel: 303-694-9130
http://www.ast.org

Liaison Council on Certification for the Surgical Technologist
128 South Tejon Street, Suite 301
Colorado Springs, CO 80903
Tel: 800-707-0057
Email: mail@lcc-st.org
http://www.lcc-st.org

Index

Entries and page numbers in **bold** indicate major treatment of a topic.

A